THE CORPORATE CRUSADERS

The
Corporate
Crusaders

A.D. Koopman

M.E. Nasser

J. Nel

Lexicon Publishers

Johannesburg

First edition, first impression

ISBN 1 86813 080 0

Cover design by W. Loots
Illustrations by P. de Zeeuw and L. Gouws
Set in 12 on 14 and 10 on 12 point Palacio
By Industrial Graphics (Pty) Ltd, Johannesburg
Printed and bound by Printpak Books, Cape

Foreword

The current state of evolution in the workplace differs in one fundamental respect from the recent past. While the period through the early eighties was characterised by reasonable stability, the mid-eighties is being impacted by a highly turbulent macro and micro environment.

In terms of the interaction between corporations and the environment, nothing is left unchallenged by this turbulence. The very core of business - the strategic direction - is being tossed and turned in a wave of restlessness. In the wake of this turbulence has come a growing alienation between management and its workforce. The fabric of the corporate environment has been torn apart. Opposite objectives, rejection of the free enterprise system, different motivations, industrial sabotage and ongoing disruption are becoming the order of the day.

It is to these issues that *The Corporate Crusaders* addresses itself. The work of Albert Koopman has by now become legendary in South Africa. In Cashbuild the results have been astounding - harmony in objectives, internal stability, labour peace, reduced shrinkage, increased productivity and a dramatic upturn in corporate profitability. Substantial by any yardstick, particularly when one recognises that all these achievements have been attained against a daunting scenario and poor performance results in the retailing sector.

A major contributor has been the removal of polarisation in the work environment via the creation of shared values between management and its people.

This book sets out to explore the secrets of this success story and more especially to share the formula for the benefits of business and the greater economy. The authors have attempted to not only report on the Koopman formula but also to conduct a sound academic evaluation of the process and its extended application to all areas of business. If this integrated approach gets the reader as excited as its authors, the benefits will be substantial.

This is a corporate crusade against limitations on vision, corporate efficiency and the alienation between management and its workforce. In this crusade, the mentoring process will form an integrated part of introducing and sustaining the new corporate culture. Not only will it accelerate the growth of the new corporate talent, but its contribution to corporate efficiency and effectiveness is more than obvious in visionary management.

All of this shift requires management courage - courage to respond to the challenges facing the corporate environment in an evolving South Africa. Whether the corporate crusade becomes the hallmark of corporate excellence depends on management's willingness to act courageously.

MARTIN E. NASSER
Professor in Organisational Change

Acknowledgements

The authors would like to thank the people whose generosity of spirit and dedicated labours are helping create a better South Africa for us all.

Our special thanks to the Tradegro group for permission to use the Cashbuild story, as well as its generous financial support.

To the many corporations whose excellent work is quoted freely throughout these pages - without them the South African corporate environment would be much the poorer.

To Sonya Stastny our thanks for the extreme care she took in preparing the manuscript; to Liz Bennett, our executive editor, for the dedication to clarity which has made this book readable; to Yvonne Kemp and all the people at Lexicon Publishers for their supreme efforts in publishing the manuscript in the shortest possible time; to Maureen Tray for the continuous coordination which has made the whole project possible; and to Vanessa Bluen and Elaine Goodman for their assistance with historical details.

Our thanks to the following corporations for their financial support in marketing this book: the Allied Group, Pick 'n Pay and Wooltru Limited.

On the home front we would like especially to acknowledge our families, corporate and personal friends as well as the Nasser Associates for their unstinting support and encouragement in turning a dream into a reality.

Contents

PART ONE

PART TWO

PART THREE

Prologue

Cashbuild was started in 1978 by the Metro Cash and Carry group, with Albert Koopman as its Managing Director. It consists of a chain of wholesale builders' merchant stores targeted, in the main, at the one-man show type of builder. The company was initially very successful. Three stores were opened in 1978, four more were in the pipeline a year later, and by 1982 there were 12 stores, while the company that year generated pre-tax profits of close on R700 000.

In 1982, however, profits began to slide. Koopman wasted no time and his investigations convinced him Cashbuild's survival and future success could be ensured only through the introduction of drastic changes to its philosophy, culture and management style. From 1983 onwards, Koopman began to reshape the company and, by 1986, full worker participation had become a reality.

This radical approach was vindicated when company profits climbed to R1,6 million in 1984, and to nearly R4 million in 1986. Late that same year (1986) Cashbuild became a listed public company. In 1987 the company opened branch number 31 at Bloemfontein, and company results published weeks prior to publication of this book continue to reflect an outstanding performance of some R5,2 million net profit before tax.

PART ONE

Koopman

1 The crisis

Cashbuild was started in 1978 after a year's research had convinced me that there was a gap in the market for building materials, which could be profitably filled by a wholesaler operating on a cash and carry basis. My assessment was that we were looking at a market of about R4 000 million per annum. It was a market that was subject to very erratic demand, and the traditional distribution channels weren't able to meet that demand. You had to have a series of warehouses that could absorb the shock of the surges in demand. A professional wholesale operator would also shorten the distribution channel — and he'd be in business to stay.

We took advantage of the low entry costs near various black territories and opened our first three stores in Kingwilliamstown, Louis Trichardt and Vryburg. By locating our operations in these areas, we also kept our overheads right down.

By 1979 these three stores were already operating on a profitable basis and a further four were being built. Pre-tax profits rose from R40 000 in February 1980 to R680 000 for the financial year end of 1982.

As far as Cashbuild's philosophy was concerned, we believed that if we concentrated on just three aspects of our business, we'd be a successful organisation. These three aspects were:

> Give value to the customer
> Be innovative and adaptable
> Be totally committed to the business and to efficient organisational structures.

The way it worked was also pretty simple and straightforward. Point number one was easy — in the early days of any business, the one and only thing you understand is that the customer is King. And the person who knows all there is to know about the customer is the boss. What he says goes. Under the whip, the service is provided.

Point number two — just as easy. The boss knows all about being innovative and adaptable. He's the creative guy. He is the guy who knows all markets. And he is the guy who tells the people what bad lines must be cut and what new lines must be added. He is also the guy who knows exactly where to change a system, even if he doesn't work with it himself.

Point number three — to be committed is, after all, what's expected. Everyone must be committed. And if the boss is 100% committed, why shouldn't everyone else be? They all understand that if the business is successful, there will be pay increases, bonuses, better conditions. Surely? So it stands to reason everyone is committed. As for organisational matters, they're a different thing altogether. They're the boss's province — what would the average worker know about such things?

That was how we did things back in 1982. That was how the boss did things back in 1982. Bless his soul in his ivory tower.

The crash of 1983

Midway through calendar year 1982 the group had 12 branches — and profits were on the slide. At the end of the financial year 1983, profits took a dive back to R600 000 pre-tax, i.e. with five new branches and a boom going on! Somewhere something was going wrong, but where?

At Cashbuild we always prided ourselves on being men of action and the time had come for *serious* action. No excuses for bad performance, just a complete re-evaluation of the status quo.

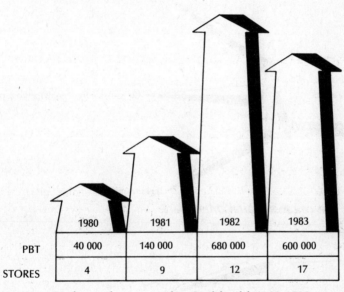

	1980	1981	1982	1983
PBT	40 000	140 000	680 000	600 000
STORES	4	9	12	17

Figure 1: Profit performance for Cashbuild 1980-1983

One of the things we had at the Cashbuild Head Office in those days was a picture of our hierarchical structure. It hung on the wall. It was something the boss had seen to. Months later, Cashbuilders would recognise that kind of thing as polishing the image, rather than greasing the wheels. Meanwhile, there it was, everyone nice and neat, each one in his own little box. No-one going anywhere. No leaders moving up, no new leaders getting in. And no new ideas, either. Just little "boxed" ideas from boxed-in people.

Rigor mortis started to set in. People started politicking and pretty soon, individual goals and values were no longer congruent with management's goals and values, and neither of the two was in keeping with the company's philosophy. The organisation had lost the singlemindedness of its early days, and now there was no "cause" to fight for. There were a lot of trained men, but no committed soldiers.

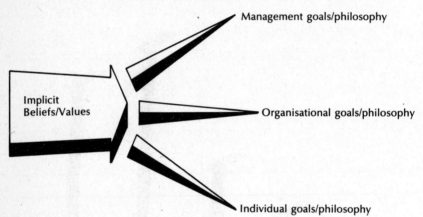

Figure 2: The organisational dilemma

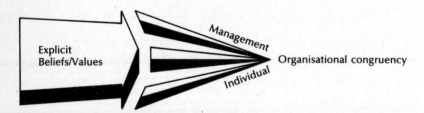

Figure 3: Organisational re-alignment

In all his wisdom, in his ivory tower and with his crystal ball, the boss had failed. At least that much was clear.

What was also becoming clear was that our <u>organisational structure was too autocratic</u>. So was my own management style. Obviously we had to change to a more democratic approach — managing by consent of the people. We had to change gear — but how? Wouldn't the people see it as "soft"?

I told myself that it isn't the blow of the sword that counts, it's more a matter of how well you know the enemy. So, the first lesson of <u>management by walking around</u> is that you have MBWA. to walk out there where the people are. It was time to ask the people: why? In those days it was the hardest thing for me to do. I felt like a puppy on the ground, belly up, waiting for my guts to be ripped out in the dog fight.

8/2.

Keep your fears to yourself but share your courage with others. (Robert Louis Stevenson)

2 The transformation

In April/May 1983 we organised three regional workshops with our managers, regional managers and head office teams. The objective was clear — "How can we improve our slipping performance?" was what we asked them.

At our June 1982 conference we had already used a Likert type scale to evaluate staff feelings toward the company and at that stage the result showed an 89% pro-Cashbuild company feeling. At the 1983 workshops the first item on the agenda was the "Corporate Culture" questionnaire (see Appendix 4). The result confirmed our "congruency slip" — it now showed a drop to 74% pro-company.

You may wonder why we regarded this result as disastrous. After all, a lot of companies are content with a 50% pro-company rating on similar scales. But in a situation where we had strong leadership, and a strong pro-company attitude, to drop to 74%

[handwritten marginal note: evaluat- of people's perceptn of c°]

was a crime. It was just not good enough. That's not how you win. And one thing I'm not interested in is mediocrity.

For two full days, each workshop dealt with questions such as:

What do you think of the boss as leader?
How do you rate your regional manager or boss?
How effective is our marketing strategy?
What about black advancement?
What do you believe we should do about training?
Do we cope with environmental change?
How do we view union activities?
What's our internal communication like?
How are we going to break across cultural lines?

And hundreds more were discussed and brainstormed. The message that came out of all of this wasn't always to my liking. For the first time, my true blue men were accusing me of being pompous, egocentric and distant. A bitter pill to swallow. Achim van Zyl from Kimberley summed it up at our Johannesburg Indaba: "Albert, when you come to my branch the ground shudders but you leave no footprints."

But even more important was the picture that was emerging of our black workers. According to the managers who were taking part in the workshops, black employees were just not motivated. The consistency with which this came up was very disturbing. Some of the things that were said:

They don't care for the company
They don't understand the business
They're badly educated
You can't train them
They won't talk or open up
You can't do anything with them.

At Cashbuild, we eventually came to the conclusion that there is no such thing as a demotivated employee. There's only a weak

7

manager who can't motivate. What some of us did know, was that by and large our black employees appeared to have a fine understanding for the interdependence of values and systems in their culture. We realised that the Cashbuild culture, with its boxed hierarchy, was meaningless to them. They just couldn't see the connection between their worth and the company's efforts. They had no "cause" because there was no reward. How simple!

Or was it? In South Africa we go for quick-fix solutions when it comes to developing people — especially blacks. We all know about the shortage of skilled labour and the management stretch — but somehow we have not been able to solve the problem of the transfer of skills. At Cashbuild we came to believe that the reason for this is twofold:

* The educational system for blacks has been hopelessly inadequate, leaving black job entrants at a considerable disadvantage in comparison with their white counterparts — not only in knowledge and skills, but in their overall perception of business.
* Blacks will never understand the purpose of business and how it functions until such time as they are given full participation in business with an accompanying right to benefit from the system materially as well as spiritually.

What we learned at Cashbuild was that in order to transfer skills, we had to start training people through the entire business structure, and to provide a culture in which human development would prosper. As we travelled along this road, we discovered as well that we had to create new structures in our business to make the journey possible and successful.

One of my firm beliefs is that here in South Africa, as in most western countries, we have separated the social man from the productive man and we pay for his capacity as a productive unit rather than his pride in labour. With this attitude you can never

8

hope to develop the whole person. A second belief is that most South African managers judge and reward their labour force by means of rank and status, something which the Cashbuild work-force said they despised. They made it clear to us that they didn't want to be treated as individuals but preferred the security of the team. An individual had to "earn the right" to be a leader before he could step out ahead of the team.

Thirdly, we South African whites are terrified of getting close to people, let alone talking to our workforce. We prefer the do-main of our ivory towers where we can be comfortable with our perceived "secure" situation. This is demeaning of self. If we believe that we white managers have "security" in our work-place then it means we view life as nothing but birth and death because we have forgotten the process of living.

But if we are committed to the process, and to improving it, we as managers have to become leaders. We have to get out of our ivory towers, "value trade" with our workforce and change our perceptions. When these barriers have been removed, only then can we start talking about a feeling of security.

A two-pronged attack

I believe a good brainstorming session should cover at least a hundred issues, and in fact most of our sessions did just that. The interesting thing was that when we categorised the issues, five key elements came up again and again. It was as if one could categorise each issue discussed, into one of the five key areas. The issues always revolved around either:

The customer
The employee
The company
The competitor/supplier
Motivation

The first breakthrough came when we realised that these five elements could give us our starting point. Surely somewhere in there a "cause" could be developed for Cashbuild. A "cause" which creative corporate crusaders could implement. A "cause" that would capture a strong employee following. I started to see that our five key elements were interdependent, and at the same time, I saw that our marketing — in fact our whole business — actually revolved around each employee. (And not the other way round.)

A second breakthrough came about as a result of the intense interaction that took place at our workshops. These, by the way, became a way of life at Cashbuild.

When you conduct a brainstorming session, you have to listen. When you listen to people you become aware of them. Day in and day out, I was confronted with people's vitality. I was experiencing their creativity. More than that — they let me see what mattered to them, what they cared about, what they dreamt about, how they lived.

If you stay in your ivory tower, you experience your people as boxes. Your organisation is just a system of rules and regulations. Even when you tell yourself it's people you're working with, and it's people who matter — it doesn't have any meaning until you get out of that ivory tower, to where the people are. When you've heard a man's heartbeats, you can never think him back into a box.

Cashbuild was actually a living organism. Alive with human spirit and human potential; waiting to be led, by a leader — not a boss.

The importance of the *team* started to mean something tangible to me: a team made up of these people, whose vitality I'd been experiencing — there could be no distinction in colour, sex, class or job categorisation. In South Africa, when we talk team, we usually don't mean "blacks as well" — and that's where we're going wrong.

We also go wrong in our leadership, somehow. True leadership must benefit the followers, not just enrich the leader. Yet

10

many Chief Executive Officers, after fighting like hell to get to the top, go into hibernation and forget that they're leaders.

Most certainly I did not want to be one of these. The need for urgent action to avoid that prompted the formulation of our two-pronged attack.

* Giving the people a holistic organisational structure interpretable by all.
* Integrating all staff right to the floor sweeper into the functioning of the business through participation.

Our new "hierarchy" — a holistic view

Our new organisational "structure" (Figure 4) could be viewed as a pyramid, consisting of the five key elements:

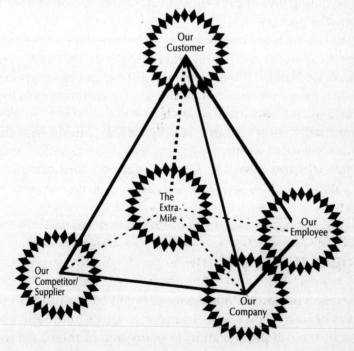

Figure 4: Cashbuild organisation philosophy

Our customer — offering value for money with total commitment and constancy
Our employee — the development of human potential as a matter of passion
Our company — to continuously seek ways of improving processes and adapting to our environment
Our competitor/supplier — to exploit all avenues for competitive advantage at all times
The Extra Mile — the key element — to pursue our goals with creativity and commitment to the "cause".

A game of soccer is a good analogy to illustrate the interdependence of these five elements. The game can't begin until you have a field (company), spectators (customers), an opposition team (competitors) and players (employees) who play to win (the Extra Mile). If any of the elements are missing, you cannot have a game of soccer.

Likewise with our organisation — the interdependence of customer, employee, competitor and company creates and gives life to the organisation. Whether the soccer team or organisation wins or loses, the game depends on the level of commitment (the Extra Mile). This is central to all.

The "will to win" in turn, is only commensurate with the rewards achievable within the organisation — recognition, money, fulfilment, self-esteem, etc. If rewards are not forthcoming, willing soldiers will be few and the cause will die.

People participation

As I have said earlier, our business revolved around the contribution of every employee. In order to drive home the importance of the full participation of every one of them, we had to spell out a few premises.

12

* It must be recognised that *every* employee is involved in the marketing process of getting the goods from the supplier to the customer.

* Quality service is achieved if the system remains constant through people, through nothing else. To improve on quality service we had to:
  Train more
  Motivate through better supervision rather than control
  Give people a say over their workplace.

* This aim of providing a quality service in the market would lead to higher productivity by:
  Changing the people who did the work
  Re-defining the way people work
  Giving job enrichment by changing the work people do.

* If the market was our "enemy" then it had to be captured and our customer satisfied by *committed people.* People needed to belong to and identify with the company's cause and philosophy.

It was people, people and more people. Through workshops we soon came to the conclusion that we had to set up a system to hear the voice of our labour force and what they felt about the "cause". These workshops were so fruitful that we decided to implement them further down the line and this was how the system of CARE Groups (Cashbuild's Aspirations with Regard to Excellence) came about.

8/2.

13

> *A problem only exists when there is a **perceived** discrepancy between where you are and where you would like to be and you do not know how to get from one place to the other.* (Edward de Bono)

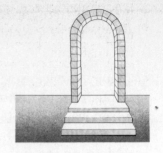

3 CARE — a whole new world

Why the CARE philosophy?

I was beginning to understand that the teaching of thinking is not the teaching of *logic* but that it has far more to do with *perception.* In our specific case, it was in essence, turning thinking about people upside down and looking at our business in a totally different manner.

At Cashbuild, we saw quite clearly what the interdependence was between our five key elements — customer, company, employee, competitor/supplier and motivation. However, we knew also that our business operated in a larger macro environment and that in today's South African environment, increasing pressures — from community groups and unions — would be brought to bear against business to act out its social role.

Traditional business has as its main objective the maximising of profits. Social responsibilities are merely by-products of the system — often viewed as the "unnecessary evil". That is rapidly changing in our current environment and I believe that big business will start executing its social obligation with a greater sense of urgency. *If it doesn't, it will not survive.*

A key objective of business is to satisfy shareholders in the process of creating further wealth. This in turn will achieve other objectives such as growth, security and employment opportunities. However these objectives cannot succeed in a vacuum and often these objectives mean nothing to the employees other than that labour is being exploited for some capitalist ideology. They see no benefit in the system. This is the perception we hoped to change at Cashbuild. And I *don't* mean that we embarked on a programme of attempting to persuade people to see things differently. I mean that we took up the challenge to change — *really* change — our business so that our people would see a different reality. And that would change their perception. The CARE philosophy would be an entrenchment of our moral and economic obligation to our employees.

What it meant was that we were all going to have to take the plunge. We were going to have to learn how to swim *inside* the pool rather than on dry land. Too often, our packaged programmes try to teach people how to swim on dry land, because in South Africa, management is genuinely afraid of entering the water!

We knew that our workforce was alienated from our system (they never understood it in the first place and never reaped the benefits from it either) and that we had to do a mighty good job to bring them into our business as "co-owners". How else could they start believing in our business other than by reaping direct benefits from it? But first we had to overcome the credibility gap.

I remember an incident at Groblersdal that brought this home to me. Kaizer Sihlangu, his accusing finger pointing one inch from my nose, asking me, "Why now, Mr Koopman? Why now after 300 years of deceit and cheating and denial of our rights in your world?" I had a problem. I had the "right" to discipline him for insolence and insubordination according to union laws, but the honest reproach in his eyes forced me to do something quite different and spontaneous. I took my jacket off and laid myself down on the ground, saying: "Do what you have to now, Kaizer, but when I get up, I'll be your leader — not your manager." Kaizer Sihlangu today is a true crusader, a loyal, fervent believer in the Cashbuild "cause".

Development of the CARE philosophy

It is difficult now to reconstruct how the philosophy evolved. By no means was it a tidy sequence of events! We went into the whole process of change without any prerequisites or preconceptions. It was an article of faith that it should be an open-ended process. There was constant discussion, managers would come up with some ideas, we'd talk to workers about them, find out what they thought. They'd come back at us with more ideas, suggestions, demands. So it went.

The following presentation of the CARE philosophy cannot convey the turbulence of all of this. Let me just emphasise again that it came about as a result of participation of workers at all levels right throughout the organisation. It wasn't bashed out overnight, or even over a few days. It took months. We'd add something here, throw out something else that wasn't working.

Ultimately, top management decided that everyone should, as a right, have a say over their workplaces; and that we would share two intrinsic principles of the forces of production — enterprise and labour.

The way we saw it, the manager could no longer be seen as the extension of the capitalist owner. He had to become part of the proletariat and part of the total *team* that was running the business. He no longer had an inalienable right over the *means* of production. Capital and land are out of reach for most black

16

people in South Africa, either through lack of resources or simply through legislation. So the only piece of the pie which they (our Cashbuild workers) could directly control was enterprise (management, policy, decision-making) and labour (human resources and skills).

There was no denying the facts of environmental pressure. We *had* to genuinely give our employees communal ownership over the means of production. Our workers had to have a *real* voice in the development of company policy and the total decision-making process. Once they had this power they would feel in charge and we believed that in this manner our business would be able to pursue its singlemindedness of purpose.

Every employee would start viewing himself as having a vested interest in the business and over time, his perception of company goals would change. (In the meantime, the company itself was being transformed.) These perceptions would continue to change, commensurate with the overall process of change and the degree of reward from the system. The commonality of the philosophy could then be effectively used as a guide for acceptable and non-acceptable behaviour within the organisation. However, at *all* times all employees had to be involved in the design of the philosophy.

The move to communal ownership over the means of production was born from necessity rather than ideology. Our employees' lack of understanding of the business system as a whole frightened us. You cannot win a war if the soldiers believe one thing and the generals have a different philosophy.

The following story will give you an idea of how the soldiers saw the system. Isaac Mpobane from Koringpunt: ''My wages come from the boss. He gets the money in two tins delivered by the green vehicle (Fidelity Guards), he buys some stocks and these get rung up on the till. Every night he takes the bags of money home. He then works out how much he owes us and pays our wages.'' Capitalism as seen through black eyes. And this, by the way, was a typical viewpoint.

CARE groups

A good leader should never shy away from conflict. Instead he should be fostering a climate where healthy conflict can actually contribute to the well-being of the organisation. (Peter Drucker)

Like a government which has built-in mechanisms for regulating the wielding of power between different groups, we had to devise a power regulator within our own organisation. We agreed that not only must we run our business according to our system, we needed to give it a tool for *just* management (or government). The current centurion type management in our business was no longer acceptable and a different power base had to be developed in order to manage more justly. Our Creed - let's sit down and talk straight, let's develop a total open-door policy - with no tigers left inside the unlocked cages!

And thus the idea of CARE groups evolved. They were designed in the first place to start bridging the immense communication gap which existed between black and white employees - at all levels. I was especially aware of that gap in Vryheid once, when a puzzled Albertnigo Mfaba asked, ''Why are you cross with me Mr Albert?'' I suppose I must have looked as puzzled as he was at that point, so he went on to say: ''You must shake hands like this'', serving me a limp handshake. To him, I was being aggressive with my firm handshake. So we learn, so we learn.

Secondly, the intention was for these groups to serve as a platform for active participation by all staff members for the well-being of the company; and thirdly, they were to start forming an internal power base for staff.

It almost seems artificial that one should have to set up specific structures in order to tackle such basic human concepts as communication and teamwork, but be that as it may.

Our vision had a time span of five years for the system to work and if we measured feelings and attitudes regularly, the model should be successful by then. So we thought, but the change was painful, and it needed thousands of kilometres and many an 18-hour day to get the message across.

CARE group structure

It must be said at the outset that the CARE groups were one of the outcomes of MBFA — Management by Fumbling Around! They served a purpose — a crucial one at a crucial time — but were later replaced by other structures.

The employee levels were broken down into five main groups and a President elected for each group by majority vote. The President's function was to interface with management on issues of common concern.

CARE GROUP I : Caddies, sweepers, tea persons, general labourers

CARE GROUP II : Goods-receiving clerks, chief cashiers, receptionists and other semi-skilled jobs

CARE GROUP III : Managers, trainers, long-term advancement trainees

CARE GROUP IV : Administrators, bookkeepers, creditors, sub-accountants, regional managers

CARE GROUP V : Chief executive officer, operations manager, buyer, finance manager, personnel manager.

The requirements were that a meeting was to be held once a month with the President and matters of common concern aired at each meeting. Members of the next highest CARE group had to be present so that problems between the different levels could be confronted.

CARE company and organisation

Acknowledging to ourselves that we are all members of one team to improve our organisation and quality of worklife, brings us clarity of purpose and a sense of relatedness as we go about our business. We are together. (Marilyn Ferguson)

Our original intention was to be innovative and adaptable, but we had soon realised, early in 1983, that the culture of the company was not conducive to innovation or adaptation. In fact, we weren't even maintaining standards, and not enough questions were being asked to find out why. Not from the right people, anyway, i.e. from the man who performed the job.

But then, why should anybody in the company contribute ideas or views if all they ever got in return was a high-handed response or a put-down? Especially in South Africa, where cultural and political chasms already exist outside the work place. We had suggestion boxes all over the place, but they were meaningless. Boxes, again. No human contact, just pieces of paper. And nine times out of ten the boss would take credit for any suggestions put forward in his division. So what was in it for the individual? We came back to the same answer yet again — we had to achieve genuine, open participation by all members if we were going to engage them in the improved functioning of our systems and business. Think tanks, brainstorming sessions, workshops, indabas — these were what we needed to deal with problems. No more suggestion boxes!

One of the first tasks that top management tackled was to redefine our organisational and corporate objectives. We came up with the summary, set out in Figure 6 (pages 22 and 23), of the process we were going through.

This outline was all very well for the ivory tower — but what about everyone else? We were all going to have to think, sleep and dream it. And everyone would be involved in making it happen. We had to present our objectives in a way that would be meaningful to everyone. To this end, we conceptualised the outline as shown in Figure 5.

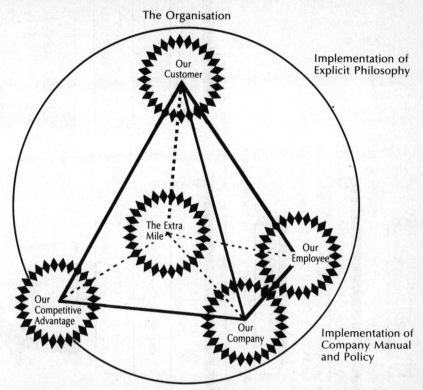

Figure 5: The new corporate pyramid

Along with this, each employee, at every level, would be given the philosophy (as designed by the people themselves), to read. This booklet was ultimately translated into seven languages. And any staff member (anyone, *including* the boss) could be reprimanded by anyone else — from the CEO to the tea person — for violation of the philosophy. Some of the key points that have been written into the booklet, for each and every Cashbuilder to see and accept and live by, are as follows:

* We are committed to a policy of joint decision-making and participation at all levels, and all individuals must play their

To determine organisational vs environmental fit. This led to the following items of concern.

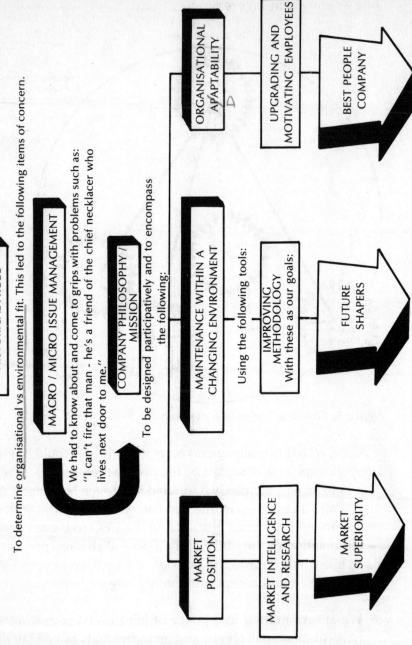

INITIAL HISTORICAL PROBE

MACRO / MICRO ISSUE MANAGEMENT

We had to know about and come to grips with problems such as: "I can't fire that man - he's a friend of the chief necklacer who lives next door to me."

COMPANY PHILOSOPHY / MISSION

To be designed participatively and to encompass the following:

MARKET POSITION

MAINTENANCE WITHIN A CHANGING ENVIRONMENT

ORGANISATIONAL ADAPTABILITY

MARKET INTELLIGENCE AND RESEARCH

Using the following tools:

IMPROVING METHODOLOGY
With these as our goals:

UPGRADING AND MOTIVATING EMPLOYEES

MARKET SUPERIORITY

FUTURE SHAPERS

BEST PEOPLE COMPANY

22

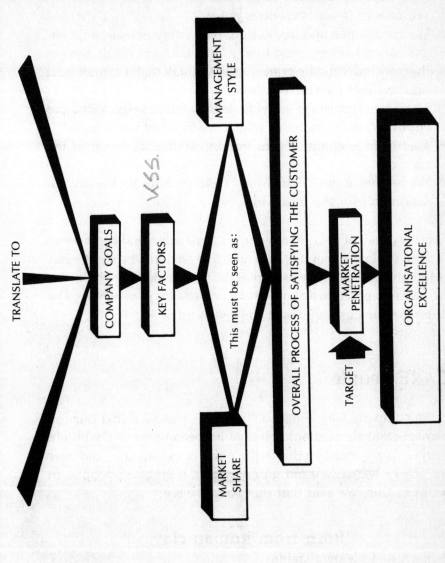

Figure 6: The stages in creating a CARE organisation

TRANSLATE TO

COMPANY GOALS

KEY FACTORS

x55.

MANAGEMENT STYLE

This must be seen as:

MARKET SHARE

OVERALL PROCESS OF SATISFYING THE CUSTOMER

MARKET PENETRATION

TARGET

ORGANISATIONAL EXCELLENCE

part in finding solutions to problems. Only in this way can we build an effective team for the maximum benefit of both the individual and the organisation.

* We believe in an open-door policy.
* We are an open and free culture with every person in the organisation having access to any line manager. We do not see that any individual's grievance is so small that it cannot land on the Chief Executive's desk.
* Our Team consists of individuals of different sexes, races and cultural creeds - none of which we discriminate against.
* Cashbuild is committed to training staff at all levels of the hierachy.
* We believe in the ''Extra Mile'' concept, both for the organisation and for the individual.

Now we could, at last, get moving! The crusade could begin, even though we knew that it would take five, six, maybe eight years before the philosophy was part of the Cashbuild way of life. But we were prepared to do something and to start somewhere. The difference at Cashbuild was that we *acted*.

CARE people

If the company was going to change, it was vital that our top management team should change its perception of Cashbuild people. We worked on this to the point of exhaustion, and over the weeks we bashed out a new way of seeing our people. In terms of this, we said that our people were:

Born from human clay

* Each had his own rights
* Each was an individual
* Each had the will to work
* Each wanted to have some control over his destiny.

Moulded with care by

* A Company that would provide a platform for <u>cross-cultural</u> <u>understanding</u>
* A Company which would genuinely <u>listen</u> to all its people
* A Company which would place <u>no limits on an individual</u> and how high he could rise
* A Company which <u>recognised human endeavour</u>
* A Company which developed <u>strong team cohesion.</u>

And functioning with pride because they

* Were <u>well-motivated</u>
* Had a sense of <u>pride</u> in themselves and their company
* Felt that they <u>belonged</u>
* Were <u>committed.</u>

Along with this new perception there grew a strong sense of urgency on the part of top management for EEO (Every Employee an Owner). The development of <u>support systems to ensure that</u> <u>rewards would be forthcoming</u> at all levels was crucial. If these failed, the entire philosophy would fail.

About the actual philosophy of EEO we had no doubts at all. Everyone wanted a meaningful say in his place of work, to feel he belonged. Everyone wanted to be a member of the team. Everyone wanted to feel a sense of ownership in the business.

If we could deliver on this, the benefits to the business would be there, no question. If as a worker I feel part of the place, then I will care for it, look after it. I'll try and see to it that the stock doesn't walk off the premises. I'll try and save money. If I feel this is my business, its profits become important to me.

CARE marketing

The important thing here was to remember the interdependence between our five key elements. And once again, a change of perception was needed. We were used to thinking of the business in a functionally differentiating manner — goods receiving, selling, invoicing, security — and so on.

An alternative view is to be had if you ask, as we did, what all these functions are about. Then you can see that they're all part of one and the same process — servicing the customer. So suddenly, instead of having six men who receive goods, six men who load goods and six men who sell goods (i.e. six men who serve the customer), you now have 18 men who are all involved in the process of servicing the customer! Not only do those 18 men now see themselves and their work differently — their managers do as well. All the attitudes begin to change.

What we still needed, however, was a competitive advantage, arising out of the CARE strategy, which would be difficult to imitate. We needed an integrated marketing system of our own. When we finally came up with it, we called it Integrated Interdependence (see Figure 7).

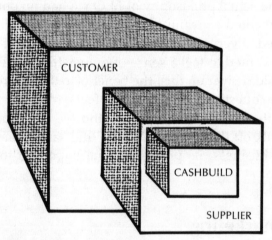

Figure 7: Integrated interdependence

The traditional view, in our market, was that the customer and the supplier were to be kept at arm's length from one another. We said "no" to that. All of us operated in the same market place, all of us depended on each other. We shouldn't be keeping our distance — we should be eating at the same table!

So we developed a system of workshops where customers, suppliers and Cashbuilders could get together and work on their problems and goals as a team. Eventually, Customer Focus groups and Supplier Focus groups became the norm, and they routinely worked out courses of action and changes in strategy to the mutual benefit of all concerned.

1984 — A year of turmoil and changing values

It seemed as though everything was happening at once in 1984. We were developing a new philosophy, working out new objectives, running groups with our customers and suppliers, and there were workshops and more workshops at every branch in the company. Most important of all, the CARE groups were meeting every month.

We asked the CARE group Presidents to record minutes of every meeting so that we could monitor, on a monthly basis, what was happening in the groups. Executives were also very active in attending CARE group meetings so that they could hear what the people were saying. It was a complete learning exercise for us all — one of the most fascinating years at Cashbuild, to say the least.

Presidents were fumbling, staff weren't contributing, managers weren't managing — we had it all. The first Presidents' Day was held in early 1984. We asked them to complete the Corporate Culture questionnaire and discovered an 81% pro-company feeling. Great! we said. You see what happens when people start sensing that they belong!

A few months later, at our managers' conference, we asked management to complete the same questionnaire and the reading for this level of staff had fallen a further percentage point to 73%. What a ridiculous situation — hyped up workers with demotivated managers! The shift of power bases was seen to be very threatening, but at least it was an internal power base and not an external one.

The importance of tea and coffee issues

I don't believe that white managers in South Africa have ever come to the realisation of just how important "tea and coffee" issues are to black workers. We are all guilty, in our pigheadedness, of viewing black workers as unimportant and inferior. And this has got nothing to do with politics. Plain commonsense humanitarianism will tell you this is a problem!

What an experience 1984 was! I felt very scared of the future if what existed at Cashbuild at grass roots level existed across the industrial spectrum in South Africa. I felt even more scared when I thought of all those ostrich-head-in-the-sand executives who were not even aware of how their workers felt towards their businesses — never mind actually doing something about it.

I know there are a host of pressures in a changing environment, but one thing I cannot accept is the way managers actually seem to abdicate when it comes to their responsibilities towards their people. Surely they must realise that they owe it to their workers to manage conflict and have their interests at heart? After all, who pays the workers? Who in the first place is supposed to look after workers' interests? The Unions? If my wife and I have a conflict of interest, do we call in mother-in-law to preside as judge? No way!

Black advancement has been very popular with managers who want to avoid conflict rather than manage it. I've often wondered whether any of these guys would consider sending their teenage

28

kids on an "Adult Advancement Programme". Somewhere in the States maybe. The kid comes back, he's learned how a bond works, what insurance policies are about, how the HP system works. And he's a year older. But the family culture hasn't changed. Dad still doesn't listen to him, Dad still treats him unfairly, and Dad still sees him as a kid. It's the same with black advancement — the culture has to be set right before anything can happen. The people — whether it's in the family or the corporate environment — have to be willing to address the tea and coffee issues, to take them seriously.

Once we had the hard data of tea and coffee issues (in the form of CARE group minutes) we were able to evaluate to what extent potential conflict situations existed in our company. Comments such as:

* Why do the whites at this branch get a half-day off and not us?
* Why at stocktakes do CARE Group II's get steak and chips and we must settle for a hamburger?
* If we're five minutes late the boss docks our pay, but why doesn't he notice when we work ten minutes overtime?
* Why must we get tea out of mugs when the whites drink out of cups?
* Our manager is very rude to us.
* Our manager treats us like children.
* Why do some people get off on stocktake days and we are forced to stay?
* Why can't the boss give us enough notice for late overtime work? He always asks us at the last minute when we've got buses to catch and he doesn't understand that.
* Why was that man fired? He was given no training.

The list goes on and on and on. Nothing to do with politics but always *perceived* as political by management.

When confronted with these issues, managers almost always saw it as political or as a personal attack and rather than manage

29

the situation, they retaliated with aggression. In South Africa, a worker never questions his white boss, and even so, the boss invariably takes an aggressive approach. Somehow it's easier to be aggressive, it keeps the boss in a comfort zone.

The sad thing, and the irony of it all, is that the manager then says to you: "But my chaps don't *want* to talk and open up to me", and he actually wonders why! And again, none of this is political — what we're talking about here is plain, old-fashioined _human dignity_. I sincerely believe that too many South African managers don't believe that black workers also have dignity.

The monitoring of "tea and coffee" issues showed a monthly average of about 56 issues per group being discussed in the CARE group structure. Next, it was up to management to respond — and we did. Whether it was a question of providing boots, giving more training, days off — we attended to the problems. By the end of the "working" year, the number of tea and coffee issue had dropped to about five a month. At last — people were being heard. But this was only the beginning.

9|2.

When you experience life as broader, richer and being more open-minded, events manifest themselves differently.
Individual events are either "successes" or "failures" and exist in content. But in context, life isn't a case of winning or losing — only the process is important. (Marilyn Ferguson)

4 The silent majority

Presidents' Day March 1985 — **Feedback Time.** This time around we regionalised the Presidents' Day in order to focus on attitudes of specific regions and to gauge whether there were any disparities between regions. If there were, we would be able to adjust our management style in these regions — maybe.

purpose of P. Day

We started with the Likert scales.

First we asked the Presidents how they felt about the general status of the CARE philosophy in their group. The results are tabled below.

Table 1: Status of the CARE philosophy - Presidents

Issue	Rating on a scale 0-100		
	N.Tvl	West	South
1. The level of involvement by all staff at CARE group meetings.	45	60	62
2. New ideas as put forward by staff members. Level of forwarding ideas.	15	54	67
3. The effectiveness with which the *Branch Manager* resolves problems raised at CARE meetings.	85	73	68
4. The effectiveness of the *Teams* in resolving their problems raised at CARE meetings.	47	69	69
5. The extent to which the *Manager and Regional Manager* really display concern and interest in CARE meetings.	95	95	89
6. The Company's actual concern about the CARE Plan.	70	75	94
7. The extent to which problems affecting their workplace are resolved *jointly* with Management.	98	74	81

Issue	Rating on a scale 0-100		
	N.Tvl	West	South
8. The effectiveness of the Branch Manager as a *leader*, in displaying distinct leadership qualities, e.g. communicating, controlling, listening, empathising, etc.	84	74	60
9. The Presidents *themselves* as leaders of their people.	80	66	73
10. "Treating humans like humans" — its actual significance at their branch.	83	67	89
11. How does *two-way* communication really work in the respective branches? (Does the manager afford his/her staff an opportunity to express an opinion and then actively listen to what is being said before replying?)	90	78	75
12. The manager's empathy with all staff (i.e. seeing it from the other man's point of view).	75	70	83
13. Attendance at CARE group meetings.	100	69	63

A list of 20 questions covering these issues was then handed out. The statements were recorded on a *Paereto* basis.

Table 2 : Presidents' Day — feedback statistics

Questions attracting most negative points

		%
1. Manager does not train properly	33/52*	63
2. We do not get involved with the hiring of staff	33/52	63
3. We do not get involved with the firing of staff	37/52	71
4. Regional Manager does not attend meetings frequently enough	37/52	71
5. CARE groups don't resolve their problems jointly	39/52	75
6. Manager does not resolve problems raised at CARE meetings	39/52	75

Questions attracting most positive points

1. We're happy working for Cashbuild	52/52	
2. We're happy about the way in which Cashbuild is being managed by the manager	52/52	
3. We're happy with the way the Company is being run from Head Office	52/52	
4. Managers treat us with respect	51/52	98
5. The people and manager work well together	47/52	90
6. People make merchandising decisions on their own	47/52	90

(*33 of the 52 participants agreed with this statement.)

General Comments
1. The manager does not appear to be managing properly — very overworked.
2. CARE Committees could clear up air of mistrust between management and group.
3. The manager spends about 65% of his time on operations and only 35% of his time on personnel and staff matters.

During the discussions, though, the group was still very sceptical as to management's intentions, but once they saw management was sincere, people opened up. The data listed in Table 3 were given to all and revealed that the CARE groups were indeed helping to stabilise staff turnover. Once they saw this success they responded to the CARE structure — frankly, openly and honestly.

Table 3: Staff turnover

Branch	JULY/JUNE 1983/84				JULY/AUGUST/SEPTEMBER 1984			
	Average Complement	Left Company	Turnover %	Effective %	Average Complement	Left Company	Turnover %	Effective %
Bethlehem	12	6	50%	50%	12	12	100%	0%
Bushbuckridge	12	15	125%	(25%)	12	0	0%	100%
Gaborone	27	26	96%	4%	27	4	15%	85%
Groblersdal	16	4	25%	75%	16	0	0%	100%
Hebron	25	29	116%	(16%)	25	0	0%	100%
Klerksdorp	11	19	173%	(73%)	11	4	36%	64%
Koringpunt	7	19	271%	(171%)	7	4	57%	43%
Kokstad	23	13	57%	43%	23	8	35%	65%
Kingwilliamstown	30	19	63%	37%	30	4	13%	87%
Mafikeng	17	9	53%	47%	17	4	24%	76%
Maputsoe	25	7	28%	72%	25	4	16%	84%
Nelspruit	14	8	57%	43%	14	8	57%	43%
Phatudi	9	8	89%	11%	9	4	44%	56%
Potgietersrus	10	8	80%	20%	10	4	40%	60%
Rustenburg	21	22	105%	(5%)	21	4	19%	81%
Queenstown	24	33	138%	38%	24	8	33%	67%
Vryheid	15	21	140%	40%	15	4	27%	73%
Vryburg	18	22	122%	22%	18	12	67%	33%
Pietersburg	20	9	45%	55%	20	8	40%	60%
Louis Trichardt	34				34			
Total number of Stores	370	297	80%	20%	370	24	26%	74%
Lichtenburg					9	N/A	N/A	
Sibasa					16	0	0%	100%
Malaita					7	3	171%	(71%)
	370	297	80%	20%	402	27	27%	73%

To put these figures in a nutshell: in 1982 staff turnover was 126%; 1983/84 — 80%. By September 1984 it was down to 27%, in April 1986 it was 9% and at the time of writing it was 7%. One doesn't have to be intelligent to understand the indirect savings from a smaller staff turnover.

Our macro/micro dilemma

With hindsight I can only say that as management we were completely ignorant and naïve regarding the feelings of our black workers. The discussions held at the second Presidents' Day weren't just to do with our business. The Presidents also unfolded their feelings about the total macro environment. They told us in no uncertain terms about the black/white interdependence problem that existed in our branches. This was indeed a breakthrough in communication — and *not* out of some textbook.

As Chief Executive Officer of Cashbuild, I read a great deal, and there was a lot of information in newsletters, magazines, news snippets and a host of other printed matter apropos of the status in the labour market and other matters concerning the general South African scene. But somehow it's OK while it happens to the other guy. Somehow it doesn't concern you. And, until the day that you can put a face to the issue, until you hear a man's voice shake with emotion while he tells it like it is, until you stand in the presence of someone whose heart is bleeding, you will *not* come to the realisation of the seriousness of the situation, not to mention the complexity of it.

Telling it like it is

Presidents poured their hearts out. Here are some of the things they said:

* "Mr Koopman, I would like to resign as President because my fellow men see me as siding with management. They're no longer carrying out my instructions."
* "I have no power. Although my people voted me in I cannot get action on their requests from my manager. He simply is not interested."
* "My manager told me the other day that he sees me as a threat and will not cooperate with me. Why should this be?"
* "How high can I climb the ladder at Cashbuild if I am not trained?"
* "I am not being trained. It appears the manager is not interested in my advancement."
* "When we have CARE meetings, our manager is never present. He just says 'carry on, it's your affair'. But we don't know how to just 'carry on'. It looks like he is scared to talk to us."
* "Our manager is unfair. He hires and fires and all the staff see that he is unfair. They have asked me to deal with him but I have not got the power."
* "We don't trust our manager. He makes many promises but doesn't carry them out."
* "We don't want to be paid for individual performance. The man who is here the longest must get more."
* "What happens to my family if I die?"
* "The manager doesn't treat us with respect. He is prejudiced against blacks."
* "The company has cheated us for so long. Why is it suddenly changing? We don't trust the company."
* "Our manager does not encourage us, just moans, never gives us feedback on how we're doing."
* "The manager does not understand my culture."

We came from these meetings totally drained and exhausted and once we had digested it all, the complexity of overcoming the problem often seemed too great. We had to think creatively, quickly. We set up a brainstorming session right there and then, and at the end of it we had a list of the major concerns:

* Give us more power
* We want to have a say over our workplace
* We want to actively participate in the decision-making process
* We want to be able to handle conflict and have a right to grievance procedures
* We want to be able to bring justice to conflict
* We want to have some of the benefits managers enjoy.

The pressure was on — *all the way.* But in the cold morning light what our Presidents wanted was nothing but fair play. We as management should have realised this long ago. In fact the one thing they were all saying and that came through loud and clear was:

Lou Standi

> *"Stand up and be counted, treat me like a human being who can actively produce for the well-being of all, and please share the rewards."*

How simple. It reminds me of the words of a wise old sage:

> *"If you give us something simple we shall not be impressed by it because we shall claim, we do it anyway! If you give us something complicated we shall be impressed by its seriousness but unable to use it because it is so complicated."*

Well, to avoid that trap you have to work with reality and not theory. Here's an interesting reality that will illustrate what I mean:

On one of my visits to our Groblersdal store, I noticed our lady Miriam dusting the shelves, her face like thunder. On returning to my office, I wrote her an "Albert the Lion" letter — the kind that ends with "Albert the Lion is unhappy" (see Figure 8). I said to her that it would be a far better world if she learned how to smile. Not only would it improve her own self-image but our customers would relate to her better. With a face like thunder she was actually proving to be of disservice to our customers. Would you believe it, Miriam framed this letter and hung it up in her tea kitchen! Who says recognition doesn't work for blacks? It's not that blacks don't respond to recognition — the problem is *we don't actually recognise that blacks are around!* (Miriam, by the way, has one of the toothiest grins I've seen.)

Whenever the C.E.O. goes on his rounds and sees anything contrary to offering value for money according to the philosophy, the incumbent is written this memo explaining the reason.
Albert the Lion is indeed unhappy.

Figure 8: Albert the Lion is displeased

Only through the unattainable does man achieve a hope worth living and changing for — and so attain himself.

5 VENTURECOMM — the loaded dice

Most certainly, we found ourselves looking at a complex picture. Staff turnover figures looked healthy, corporate culture readings were improving, morale was high. But the Presidents were unhappy, the CARE groups weren't working, and people were disappointed and frustrated.

We could have thrown in the towel then I suppose. My guess is that most management teams in South Africa would have done just that — and hammered another nail into the coffin of worker participation. We didn't throw in the towel. We thought about the one thing the Presidents were saying: "Do it. Do it all the way." And we took the most important decision of our lives — to go on, and to go all the way with participation. If it meant developing a black management team, we would do it. If it meant searching for the black man who could be our first black director, from the ranks, we would do it. If it meant sharing profits, we would do it. And if it meant giving workers the power to fire managers? *Yes — we would do that, too.*

Problem number one. How were we going to develop a structure which was equitable to all — one that could cope with black aspirations, advancement, power, justice and the like?

"Works Committees" — suggested the CEO, hopefully.

"Ha, ha" — said the crowd.

That dealt with the Works Committee suggestion.

According to the Presidents, works committees were management puppets. They distanced managers from the workforce even further. People weren't elected to works committees on a democratic basis, therefore they didn't help the manager *listen* to the people because they had no power base. Even CARE Group I, II, III, etc. was seen as a hierarchical system — some individuals more important than others. No, whatever we did, this *had* to be a **team** effort.

We then set out a definition of what we actually wanted and arrived at this broad concept:

> *We need a platform for genuine management involvement by all staff through a process of joint decision-making and participative management at all levels. Effective communication, training and time management thus implemented, will lead to an era of trust building through developing unparalleled company commitment by the team as a whole.*

Please cast your vote — is this what we as a company say we actually need for achieving our mutual objectives? Fifty-two out of 52. Full score for the concept.

Establishing VENTURECOMM

Now *how* to do it. Issues were again brainstormed and again a few premises had to be reshaped:

* **Eliminate in our organisation anything and everything to do with racial discrimination.**

* Implement immediately a policy of fair terms and conditions of employment.
* Give everyone an equal chance to be able to aspire to the top.
* Set up a fair grievance procedure — designed by all parties and based on the principle of freedom of association.
* Initiate, on a large scale, a comprehensive training programme.
* Encourage blacks to move into skilled jobs and develop supervisory capabilities.
* Improve the quality of life of all employees outside the work sphere through active community involvement.
* Give everyone a role in developing company policy and allow everyone to have a say over matters concerning our working lives.
* Allow everyone access to company results and performance standards.
* Respect human dignity and individual freedom of speech and rights.

A tall order. But what a challenge! We'd asked for open communication, and here we were, in the thick of it. The magnificent thing was that no-one acted like a tiger (''come talk to me and I'll bite your head off''). The result was that views and feelings just poured out as, for the first time in their lives, our workers could say what they wanted without fear of reprimand.

Above all, the cry (in between the lines) was:

* Drive out fear (of being fired, humiliated, cheated)
* Build trust
* Break down communication barriers
* Eliminate management by numbers
* Remove anything that hinders our hourly worker's sense of pride of workmanship
* Be totally committed to the cause and take a genuine interest in all employees

* **Don't rank us according to levels of importance — we must all be committed soldiers.**

Team! Team! — I want to belong to a *team*, I want the manager to be part of the *team*. Now, we all knew that there were skills and educational discrepancies and a generation and a half of inferior education you don't just bridge overnight. But we had to start somewhere with the transfer of skills.

We proposed that a mixture of what we called the hard and soft variables of the business be managed at branch level by the four most capable people elected by the CARE groups I and II, with the Branch Manager as an appointed member. Each member would hold a Portfolio of the key areas of our endeavour which we itemised and categorised as follows:

Hard Variables : Operations Portfolio

Soft Variables : Safety
Labour
Merchandise
Quality of Worklife

Assimilation and interpretation of the hard variables of the business had to remain the domain of the most skilled person, viz. the manager. Apropos of the soft variables there was really no problem. Most of our people in the semi-skilled arena could manage those. So we said — give them the opportunity to participate.

It looked as though we finally had the structure whereby the new culture could be governed. These five people were to get together on a weekly basis to discuss matters of common concern and to take decisions on the running of the branch. No different from a manager delegating tasks to specific staff, except that there was a difference regarding the power base.

We called this body of people VENTURECOMM (meaning a new way of communicating). A conceptualisation of how we thought it would work is given in Figure 9.

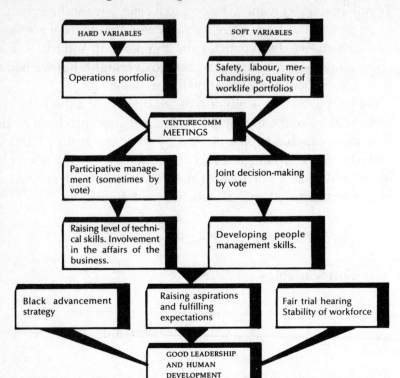

Figure 9: The VENTURECOMM process

Certain powers of VENTURECOMM were proposed:

* All hiring and firing of staff to go via VENTURECOMM (by vote); no longer the sole domain of the manager.
* Job allocation, training and personnel movement to be decided on by VENTURECOMM (by vote).
* VENTURECOMM members could vote against other team members through a system of "no confidence", i.e. if they found performance lacking. This was to *include* the manager.

Establishing trust

When we realised that the element of trust was still missing between management and labour, approval of this system had to be obtained by vote from the *entire* labour force. Presidents were therefore requested to put forward a proposal to all staff so that they could decide whether the joint "management" committee could work. They were given ten days to gather their votes and with the proposal accepted or rejected, our managers would then have the right to vote on its implementation.

From the managers' point of view it was easy. A time study analysis of their jobs highlighted the fact that they were not spending sufficient time on the soft variables of the business. A majority of 92% of the non-management staff cast their vote in favour of the system, with the managers showing a full house vote at their national rally.

Incidentally, at the national rally of May 1985 the Corporate Culture reading shot back to 84% pro-company. The attitudes of managers, regional managers and head office staff showed we were regaining our ground as a committed team and the results were starting to speak for themselves.

With the entire company now supporting VENTURECOMM by virtue of consultation and a democratic vote we were confident that:

* Our managers would become *more professional* in their approach and have more time to do strategically necessary things rather than to worry about the mechanisms of the business (especially the soft variables).
* VENTURECOMM would immediately raise the *level of aspiration* of all staff, as anyone could now aspire toward being directly involved in the running of the business and be trained accordingly.
* We would be building bridges of *trust and communication*. Two commodities desperately needed, not only in Cashbuild or

the corporate world generally, but also in the broader South African context.

* The spirit and faith with which VENTURECOMM was being implemented could only be strengthened by mature *adapted values* on the part of all parties concerned. The loyalty that was being manifested, and the growing congruency between the Company's belief and philosophy and those of its employees, were of paramount importance.

VENTURECOMM was on its way to becoming a revolutionary method of managing a business in South Africa. It would soon be established as our own home-grown, South African variety of Japanese-style management where:

* Total management participation by all was the minimum standard.
* Profit sharing was the order of the day.
* Expectations were being fulfilled.
* Human dignity took precedence over all other matters that concerned employees.

The only areas needing attention after the election of all the VENTURECOMM members (some 105-odd people), were the nuts and bolts of the system, our grievance procedures and a suitable training programme.

Once again, Cashbuild-style, four workshops of approximately 25 people each were invited to come and determine the future.

6 Power to the people

I once asked one of our groups of employees, at a typical Cash-build workshop: "If I, as a white guy want to lead you not manage you, what would you like to see me do?"

The first thing they said was "The car you drive is very high-level capitalist, but the stuff you talk isn't. You're talking our world, and that's wrong, to drive that car, it's from the wrong world." So we sold the Merc and got a Star Wagon instead.

They also said "Walk among us". And that I did too. If one of our people asked me to have supper in his home, I went. If it meant squeezing into a one-roomed home, or if it meant sitting down inside a tin shack in Gazankulu (as it once did) to a meal of donkey meat which we ate with golden knives and forks — I went!

Change is an awesome thing for most people and I believe that it is a leader's responsibility to help people accept change. Most executives in South Africa are content to wallow in opulence because "I'm alright Jack" and few even attempt to help their employees with the change process. It is this very change process which should be management's greatest challenge. Let's face it, the South Africa of today is vastly different from that of ten years ago and from that which we expect ten years hence. If the leaders and captains of industry can't provide helpful guidelines for meaningful change, we cannot blame employees for approaching a third party, such as the unions, to facilitate change. It is my firm belief that a number of South African managements have abdicated their responsibilities to their employees and somehow seem to prefer the disruption of strikes and lockouts. They seem to *want* to be immobilised when approached by their people on matters of humanitarian concern — they'd rather call the cops, which in turn only aggravates the issue.

I think the main point of concern that I'm expressing here has to do with the old, old story of "Violation of Each Others' Rights"

Violation of rights

The *company's* rights are sacred — but violation of *individual* rights, well, that's something different. (Refer to the comments earlier of docking pay for being five minutes late but not rewarding ten minutes' overtime.)

This is exactly what gives rise to conflict because each one's rights are born from two different sets of values. The amazing thing is that the conflict can revolve around basic issues like teacups. Where else in the world would you get people going on strike because a manager raises hell when a worker drinks the tea he has sent back to the kitchen?

Our South African managers immediately interpret the situation as political because of their mistaken belief that the privileges they enjoy are theirs by right, whereas the employee is only trying to assert his human dignity.

Figure 10 shows this anchored within a motivational framework.

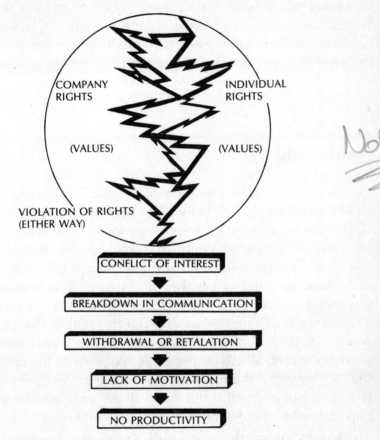

Figure 10: The infringement of company and individual rights

We believe strongly that in South African industry at large, the single biggest contributing factor to low productivity is the business of "tea and coffee" issues which impinge on individual rights and seemingly transgress managerial privilege. The worker cannot maintain his dignity under an autocratic management and will definitely not feel committed to productivity — no matter what.

49

The sadder picture is that when the unions take up the fight for individuals' rights, management sees them as the "enemy" and this mindset brings about even lower productivity. Why managements in South Africa don't get closer to their unions heaven only knows. If it has worked in Germany and Japan why not here? Are there that many faint hearts where there should be lions?

Value trading

Let me remind you for a moment of the ritual of courting which most couples go through before they get married. I'm sure most of you are familiar with the long evenings of discussion about likes and dislikes, what's right and what's wrong, about beliefs and ideals. This is nothing other than "value trading" in order to understand what makes the other person tick. Similarly at Cashbuild — before we went into partnership with our employees we dealt with the issues of rights, privileges and values by value trading. Four days per session with each VENTURECOMM portfolio holder, all 105 of them. We spoke about the beliefs of the company and the rights of the company. We spoke about industrial labour practice and above all we spoke about the feelings, attitudes, needs and rights of our employees.

There they were, eyes filled with expectation but not letting go of their values and rights; for the first time totally for the company in which they *believed* and actually helping to shape its destiny.

There was an unexpected bonus in it for me. I discovered I was working with a bunch of outstanding, wonderful people. The warmth and openness of our black employees were quite incredible. For me it was a peak experience, and I regard myself as a lucky man to have been exposed to this sort of communication. Other CEO's honestly don't know what they're missing.

Basic, *basic* communication and human understanding and sharing. It's so simple, yet it eludes us all.

Getting back to the "violation of each other's rights" issue, isn't this exactly why we need government and laws in a country? Now surely what we're saying here is the same thing except on a micro level. If, due to a clash of values, there are potential conflicts which could be disruptive in our business sphere, we actually need laws and a "governing" body — not a consulting body such as a union. This is indeed what VENTURECOMM is — a mini-government. It was out of this context that the "VENTURECOMM CREED OF TRUST" (see appendix) was born.

Voting and the appointment of portfolio holders were to be done on a *democratic* basis and as far as grievance procedures were concerned (see Fair Trial), VENTURECOMM as a body would "govern" equitably and justly. We made a distinct difference between "managing" the hard variables and "governing" the soft variables.

This was totally in keeping with our view of giving the people a say (and control) over the means of production.

Ironically enough, this say over the means of production, accompanied by freedom of speech, took precedence over wage levels. Not one of the 105 members said that wages/salaries should be on the priority list. The top concern of all was "human dignity and the respect of individual rights." In every case, each 4-day workshop confirmed this.

What the workers were actually saying here is that they would give up their jobs rather than have their human dignity or self-respect affronted. This takes the wind right out of management's sails. *It means we haven't even got job security as something to bargain with. It also leaves us with no choice but to participate.*

Once this got through to us at Cashbuild, the rest was straightforward — a matter of listing the grievance procedures and ensuring that the following rules applied:

* Anyone who violates any matter regarding the philosophy, from the CEO to the sweeper, can be "judged" and "tried"

51

by the team and corrective action taken.
* Everyone in the company must know what the company's rights are and how the individual fits into that framework vis-à-vis his own rights.
* *Top* management to react immediately in cases of dispute.

Negotiating individual and company rights is of fundamental importance, and leads to a deeper understanding of human nature and how humans behave when these rights have been violated or upheld. This has manifested itself over and over again in Cashbuild and here a specific branch comes to mind.

At Pietersburg all employees "value trade" on Saturday mornings in what are known as "Hanna, Hanna" sessions (talk outs). Everybody opens up to everybody else and all the most minute grievances get handled, there and then. From the most specific to broader issues: "Jane, you don't smile enough"; "Mr Manager your office is too untidy"; "Joseph, take a bath more frequently"; "Abraham, you're working against the team". Openness is the key. Normally individuals will keep all the little points of irritation to themselves, because of the inherent fear of confronting other individuals. But in a "herd" situation they feel a strength in numbers. In this situation of "collective" moaning, unbelievable motivation is achieved. They all air their views and get rid of their frustrations. It's like mass group therapy! Very healthy — but *someone must be listening.*

"Value trading" is extremely important for interpersonal relationships and most certainly is the best starting point for good communication, especially across cultural lines.

If "value trading" sees the beginning of a long marriage to your spouse, can it not also usher in a long relationship between boss and staff? Value trading is a human need and a fundamental right.

Threshold of discomfort for change

Fear of the unknown is a formidable inhibitor of action, it kills the spirit and deadens the imagination, and more often than not can immobilise us to such an extent that we simply cannot manage change. It is not my purpose to explore the reasons for fear. Suffice it to say that we can either be reactive or proactive in our approach to change. The obvious route is one of resistance to change because if we stay with what we know, then we stay inside a comfort zone. Either that, or we react to change from what we think is the strength of our managerial position. The reality, however, is that change eventually overwhelms us, because we usually react only once the forces at work in our known, familiar world have brought us to a threshold of discomfort. Crisis management and quick-fix models then have to be sought to cope with the change, often resulting in *ad hoc* plans which fail or solutions that are of short duration.

Once you are able to recognise and deal with problems of perception as and when they arise, and when you have a vision of what the future could be — then you can both anticipate change *and* manage it, when it happens, through leadership.

> *It is one of the most beautiful compensations of this life that no man can sincerely try to help another without helping himself.* (Ralph Waldo Emerson).

7 Casting your bread upon the water

The VENTURECOMM system was in place early in 1985. CARE groups continued to function, but were organised along different lines. The various levels and the Presidents system were done away with, and all the workers at a given branch now belonged to the branch CARE group, the basic unit of the team. VENTURECOMM decisions were discussed with the CARE group, and concerns expressed by the CARE group were taken up and dealt with by VENTURECOMM.

Soon it was time to test the water again. We had made a promise with regard to training, but first we had to find out just what the training needs were. We appointed the InterFace Project* as independent consultants, and their first step was to send in a team of completely impartial interviewers to find out how things were working out.

---

*The InterFace Project was initiated in the late 1970's by Norman Nossel, Chairman of the Adcock-Ingram Group, and Dr Melvin Sorcher, a leading consultant in behaviour modelling in the USA, as a pilot project to establish whether behaviour modelling training could be used to improve the behaviour and attitudes between white supervisors and black employees.

Here we highlight some of the problems which we encountered with the implementation of both the CARE groups and VENTURECOMM.

Problem 1

BLACKS' LACK OF UNDERSTANDING OF HOW A BUSINESS FUNCTIONS

There was no way in the initial stages that blacks saw any benefit working for Cashbuild, even less the need for participation. It was essentially a white-owned business and therefore, as they saw it, no reward would ever be forthcoming. This was gradually overcome through training, through lectures to explain how and why profits are made, how our business functioned — and of course over time, people had more and more reasons for trusting the company and becoming part of it.

Problem 2

THE CHASM OF MISTRUST BETWEEN WHITE MANAGERS AND BLACK WORKERS

Because of the almost subconscious belief that blacks are inferior, a lot of easy promises were made to them by some of our white managers regarding pay increases, overalls and other tea and coffee issues, which were never fulfilled. This was either because there was no follow-up or just plain lack of respect on the manager's part. But you can't bluff an employee and get away with it. The urgent need for a well-planned company policy and philosophy was revealed by dealings such as these.

Problem 3

THE CLEARCUT PHILOSOPHY AND POLICY WAS AT FIRST SEEN AS A THREAT TO THE MANAGER'S JOB

Managers believed that so-called "decision-making" was being removed from their domain. They saw themselves as door openers and as no longer having any "right of control" over staff and other matters. This demotivated them.

55

Problem 4

<u>THE MANAGER FEARED THE REMOVAL OF HIS POWER BASE WITH THE INTRODUCTION OF PRESIDENTS</u>

This perceived loss of power resulted in a lot of managers actually relinquishing their people matters, first to the Presidents and, later, to VENTURECOMM. As one President told us at a rally: "Our branch is run like one of the Homelands."

Problem 5

<u>MANAGERS SAW THE CARE PHILOSOPHY IMPINGING ON THEIR POLITICAL BELIEFS</u>

In the beginning, some managers worked *against* the philosophy, attempting to assert that "I am still the boss". They couldn't let go of their centurion style. Ironically these were the branches where we experienced the most labour turbulence — and the managers couldn't see it. "Freedom of speech" on the business premises was a bit too much for them to handle, so they never heard anything useful!

Problem 6

<u>BLACKS CAN'T FIRE OR REPRIMAND BLACKS</u>

Their community life somehow immobilised them against taking action against their "next door neighbour". This they feared more than anything else.

Problem 7

<u>CARE GROUPS PERCEIVED BY THE WORKFORCE AS NOT BEING AN EFFECTIVE TOOL TO "RIGHT THE WRONG"</u>

This was a definite retaliation — to centurion-like managers. These managers "bulldozed" all discussions and then people wouldn't talk openly.

Problem 8

<u>PRESIDENTS WERE PUPPETS, SIDING WITH MANAGEMENT</u>

Victimisation in reverse. We had many Presidents who wanted

to resign as a result of this victimisation. They felt that they were losing touch with their peers and being branded as sellouts.

Problem 9
TARDINESS IN GETTING THE PHILOSOPHY OFF THE GROUND
It took us three full years before we could even say that we truly had an open-door policy. Building trust was the most difficult task in getting the philosophy to work.

Problem 10
INITIALLY BLACK EMPLOYEES HAD DIFFICULTY IN IDENTIFYING WITH THE COMPANY'S ''BLACK ADVANCEMENT'' POLICY
They'd heard it all before — promises and more promises. Until they saw the genuineness of management's intent, there was no belief that any changes would really benefit them.

Problem 11
THE COMPANY FAVOURING BLACK EMPLOYEES AND FORGETTING ABOUT THE WHITES
Initially when all the ''wrongs'' had to be ''righted'', there was an over-concentration on black employees.

The only way in which we could handle these issues was through a systematic approach to training, exposing and creating awareness among our employees as to the realities. Environmental and demographic issues were always discussed with our white managers at our national rallies in order to broaden their understanding of the social, political and economic realities facing South Africa. That, together with leadership training, made them feel more comfortable with the task at hand. I'm not saying we turned them all into radicals! What they did in their private time and in their own homes was — of course — not our concern. As long as they treated one another with respect in the workplace — as long as they followed the Cashbuild philosophy at work — we were happy.

Training programmes

People at Cashbuild most certainly by now knew how to open up at indabas, workshops, seminars and the like. They knew someone would listen to them, and they started growing more confident. But communication skills were still seriously lacking. Managers weren't good at reprimanding staff ("wat maak jy daar jou blerrie kaffir?") and staff weren't good at coming back without getting aggressive ("cheeky"). CARE groups and VENTURECOMM needed to move on from the "hanna hanna" phase to more of a problem-solving mode, but they didn't really know how to.

We realised we ourselves couldn't handle the massive training programme this would involve, so we appointed outside consultants (in this instance the InterFace Project) to address the problem. They came up with the following integrated strategy, which we accepted in toto:

* Regional managers, branch managers, supervisors, VENTURECOMM members and employees to be given practical skills

in communicating effectively with each other in difficult situations at work.

* Managers and VENTURECOMM members to be given practical skills in leading group discussions effectively, and all employees practical skills in group problem solving.
* Branch managers to be given the support and skills to handle their changing roles effectively.
* "Supervisory" problems to be reduced (this to be measured by means of responses to structured interviews).
* The amount of feedback given on work performance to be increased at all levels (measured by means of structured interviews).
* Managers and supervisors to increase the amount of on-the-job training and coaching undertaken (records to be kept at branches).
* Improvement in manager-employee relations to be measured by a 5-point rating scale in structured interviews.
* Improved teamwork to be measured by ratings given in structured interviews.
* CARE groups:
  To move from discussion of employee grievances to improving quality and efficiency of work
  To increase employee participation in CARE group meetings
  To increase the number and quality of suggestions and ideas raised by employees
  To increase speed and success of action and follow-up on CARE group issues.
* Customer service:
  To improve the quality and speed of customer service
  To reduce customer service complaints
  To give sales caddies skills to handle and respond to customer criticism.

All employees were taught how to communicate down the hierarchy, but much more important they were also taught how to communicate upwards. This would go a long way towards sorting out some of the problems the Presidents had raised. As usual, there was total involvement in the programme. Model films and videos and slides were made, and once the training sessions had started, InterFace chose a number of Cashbuilders who were then trained to eventually take over the programme. With the result that it has become a permanent, ongoing part of the overall process at Cashbuild. Part of the new culture.

In addition to this, we had told our people that anyone who wanted to move up the organisation would be given the necessary technical training to do so. A tall order, but we had to make good on it. We set up a training department and developed our own programme which we called "Learner Controlled Training". Here, you start off by completing a "competency modelling statement", which means you decide what your goals are, how high up you want to go. Then you work out what modules you have to work through to get there from where you are now. After that it's over to you. We developed a complete set of manuals for each job type, the idea being for people to work through them on their own. The manuals are very practical, each section tells you exactly what you will be able to do by the time you finish it. One of the things I firmly believe is you must give people all the support they need, but then it's up to them. I don't feed anyone else's monkey.

We South African managers are all too often guilty of overlooking the fact that we have to deal with the whole person. My experience at workshops and indabas and Presidents' Days changed my perception in this regard for good. Never again could I see a man I worked with as just a sales caddy. No - this is Promise Mpetshene and he is struggling to keep his kids fed and at school. This same Promise Mpetshene later stood up at a mass rally in one of the townships and told the SAWU officials and the people just why Cashbuild shouldn't be boycotted.

You can never hope to get that kind of loyalty, especially with our kind of macro environment here in South Africa, if you don't have a holistic approach. Time and again our workers said to us, "Treat us like people." That's what so many of the "tea and

60

coffee'' issues were about. If a man walks three kilometres to the fish and chip shop to buy his lunch, arrives to find the bus has just offloaded ten people who join the queue before he does, and he then gets back to work five minutes late, is this a worse crime than when the manager goes to lunch with a supplier and comes back at three o'clock all happy and pink-eyed? It all depends on your approach, whether you're seeing the people as human beings or as workers.

Similarly with training, it isn't enough to teach people how to do a job. You have to find a way of helping them to develop as people as well. This need which I perceived was what made me devise a course I called ''Goal Source'' to help people look at themselves in the longterm and make some key decisions in their lives as a whole.

Rebellion against your handicap gets you nowhere, self-pity gets you nowhere, one must have the adventurous daring to accept one's self as a bundle of possibilities and undertake the most interesting game in the world in making the most of one's best. (Harry Fosdick)

8 VENTURECOMM and motivation

The manager cannot motivate employees but he can develop an environment within which self-motivation becomes a reality. At Cashbuild we believed that this environment was created once we started giving our employees a say in their workplace. We had to spell out that quality of work lies in the hands of the workers and not management, and the commitment to improve standards would flow from control over such standards by the worker. Management must in turn show its commitment to employee participation by helping to solve problems and adding innovative improvements. If these two elements are missing, the full potential of the workforce cannot be developed and there will be no commitment.

The workforce normally has enormous potential but South African managers unfortunately often take the view that em-

Note

ployees are non-creative, non-productive and idle. At Cashbuild we said yes, workers will be all those things, but this is the *result* of *indifferent* management, rather than of employee choice or the inherent nature of the worker.

The need for involvement

Workers like to feel part of the business. Few things are more demeaning to a human being than calling him by his payroll number. During our three years of research we found that our employees:

> like being involved in business matters
> like to be part of management meetings
> like to be able to control the enrichment of their jobs
> like sharing in the profits
> like contributing toward the improvement of business processes.

Contrary to popular South African belief, the employee likes having a goal to work towards. The only problem in South Africa is that we businessmen actually stand in his way. We don't allow him to show or offer his full potential at his workplace. If we talk about productivity and motivation, we usually harp on the idea that it is management which causes the productivity — not the worker. In fact, South African management is the guilty party when it comes to low productivity. Not the worker, and not his union. We've learnt this lesson from hard experience and through many hours of consultation at all levels of our workforce.

Most textbook theories are taught in a vacuum with absolutely no practical participation by the workforce. This is just not adequate. Man does not work in a single dimension, he operates as a multidirectional being with needs, expressions, desires

63

and goals. Participation and sharing in the system improve his immediate environment and stimulate his personal development and aspirations. He takes pride in his work which in turn results in a visible contribution to the company — however small. Isn't this what productivity and motivation are all about?

Shrinkage and motivation

Shrinkage: the blight of retail business. The polite word for thievery - on the part of customers, staff, management or a permutation of the three.

What does shrinkage mean? When you look at it, as managers almost invariably do, from a narrow, mechanistic point of view, all it means is money straight off the bottom line. This I would be the first to endorse. But when you start to see the people involved in your business as multidirectional beings, then shrinkage starts to take on additional meanings. I eventually came to the conclusion that in many, many instances, shrinkage is the workers' vote of no confidence in the manager. So one way of dealing with the problem is to give the people another way of voting. This we did with VENTURECOMM. Most certainly, matters improved, especially at branches where there had been problems with managers.

But even 0,4% off the bottom line is too much - especially when that adds up to R600 000. *I* knew, and top management knew, what shrinkage means in terms of the well-being of our company and our employees. But did anyone else have the same perception as we did? Obviously not.

So, Cashbuild style, it was time for action. We said to everyone: ''This R600 000 is how much money we think we will have to write off this year because of shrinkage. Rather than just throw the money away, we are prepared to give you, our employees, every cent you can save on the R600 000 by reducing shrinkage.'' We followed this up with a campaign to make people aware of

64

the problem and tell them what they could do to improve matters. And we kept reminding them of the R600 000.

The results were interesting, to say the least. We gave our employees a cheque for R97 000 at the end of that year. More important, we found we had changed the organisational culture with regard to shrinkage. People continued to be aware of the problem as never before, and during that year they developed new patterns of behaviour around the issue, which carried over to the future.

result

Support systems

At Cashbuild we have in fact developed a total support structure for our corporate culture. Again, I emphasise that this wasn't something we sat and analysed and came up with overnight. It evolved - as we went round the branches, talked to people, responded to their needs and the company's needs, and as the whole participative process started to get under way - so we would come up with new ideas, new demands that had to be met, new problems that were being created by the process itself. Some of the elements of the support structure are now described.

* *Top management were completely committed* to the CARE plan. This was something people knew beyond any shadow of doubt. We said it and demonstrated it at every opportunity.
* Top management were actively involved in the follow-up of the CARE plan. We attended CARE group meetings, we read the minutes and gave the branches feedback on them, we initiated feedback sessions and interviews and questionnaires. Again, it was a highly visible involvement.
* Infrastructural communication lines were set up in order for top management to react to problems quickly. The last thing

we needed was to lose credibility because people weren't able to communicate with us speedily and effectively. This was where our open door policy was of vital importance. Every single person in the company knew that if he couldn't get satisfaction by using the usual communication channels, he could phone the CEO direct, and he would get a hearing. And action.

* A *top and line management mindset* that this is the only route to take if we want to develop one total workplace and fulfil worker aspirations and expectations.

* A total training programme: InterFace courses to develop communication; competency modelling statements and learner control training to put people on track as regards their career paths; and Goal Source to develop their human potential. This was reinforced in any and every way we could think of, at seminars and workshops, through special meetings to discuss, for example, the findings of Project Free Enterprise, through articles in our house magazine *Team News*, and even through "Albert the Lion" letters.

* A total reward system. We had bonus schemes, inter-branch competitions on anything from product displays to profitability, merit awards, "extra mile" cheques which were used on an *ad hoc* basis to give on-the-spot recognition for any unusual effort or achievement. One of VENTURECOMM's major tasks was to come up with a remuneration package which would allow staff to participate in profits, while still satisfying the claims of other parties, like shareholders, to a share of the profits.

Reward doesn't have to take the form of monetary recognition only. In fact, it shouldn't. Other kinds of recognition are just as important if not more so (we got this from our own employees as well as from Herzberg). So we also made a big fuss when someone became a "Cashbuild Pioneer" after five years' service - with an announcement in *Team News*, a personal letter, a certificate. We remembered people's birthdays, we made a fuss about merit awards and put winners' photographs in *Team News*, and people who gave consistently outstanding contributions to the organisation had their name put up in gold letters in our "Hall of Fame" at Head Office.

Get-togethers also helped build a cohesive team spirit. So we found on the many occasions when we socialised at functions like the opening of a new branch, the announcement of improved sales at branch level or a celeberation by the winner of a competition.

The pay-off

In plain and simple English, when you involve the people, the people become committed. South Africans talks, with much anxious fervour, about the free enterprise system. All too often, they complain that people aren't enterprising enough and they say that's why we have a productivity problem. I say to them, that you have to free the people to be enterprising.

I can quote you dozens of examples to prove my point; here are just a few. In the early days at Cashbuild, I spent 18 months writing manuals to try and motivate staff. They were a work of art, and a survey later showed that they were read by about 15% of the staff. Yet, when we brought out the CARE philosophy, in which everyone had had a say, we discovered that everyone, but everyone, knew the philosophy inside out. In fact, the people who couldn't read had found someone who could read it to them out loud, and they could *recite* the philosophy word for word.

Freedom means responsibility; in other words people who are free to be enterprising are also accountable. Once our people become accountable for sales and profitability, they became motivated beyond our wildest expectations. Israel Mathiba was just one of the many workers who wanted to be a Cashbuild Winner. So how did Israel Mathiba spend his annual leave? In the bush, looking for people who were potential customers, telling them to bring their business to Cashbuild. What he said to them was this: "Cashbuild are good to their staff. They're good to their customers. You can trust Cashbuild."

Take the problems we had with staff selection. At one time, we were forever sending out memos nagging people to follow set procedures — getting references, checking that people could do what they said, interviewing, etc. Part of that problem fell away when staff turnover came right - we just didn't have to replace people that often anymore. On the other hand, we were opening new branches and expanding existing stores, so we still had to find new people. They were mostly for lower level vacancies - sweepers and cleaners - because of our policy of promoting from within. The branch manager's idea for a selection interview, more often than not, was to take a look at all the applicants, see who had the biggest muscle and the least bloodshot eyes and take him on. When we started to involve people in the soft variables, the manager talked about vacancies with everyone working at the particular branch. They then decided what kind of person they needed, and then the staff themselves did a search. Turnover of new staff - always a high percentage - fell dramatically, new people took less time to settle in, and we started getting the kind of people we wanted.

Needless to say, it's the bottom line that counts. Back in 1982 our people, along with most other workers in South Africa, had no idea at all how a company utilises its profits. They thought it all went straight into the pockets of management. Educating our staff as regards basic business principles was a slow and painful process. It never really got off the ground until people started to realise they could trust management and the organisation, but when they saw that there *was* something in it for them when extra profits were generated, then the lessons and lectures and information sheets began to make sense. This effort eventually reaped a lot of benefit.

But in the end, it is our balance sheets that tell the story of workers' participation at Cashbuild more eloquently than any other attempt could hope to do. I invite the sceptics to consider that story.

*The leverage to productivity is created when the leadership within a company recognises the interdependence of individuals, their interdependence within functions and then **actively involves each** individual in a participative manner in matters affecting their lives.*

9 Managerial issues — our current status

People have often asked me how exactly it came about that our productivity at Cashbuild was so dramatically affected by this *total people participation* philosophy. This is not an easy one and I believe that for the uninitiated a brief background is necessary as to the "organisational" Cashbuild — the picture beyond the internal industrial relations process, as it were. The philosophy may have worked for Cashbuild but how transferrable is it to other organisations?

Leadership

To start with, I believe we have to look at the leader closely and try to profile him.

Profile of leader.

Prerequisite 1

He needs to be value driven (and not at buzz word level either). He needs to display in his daily life his obsession with achieving the highest standard for the organisation. If he comes in at nine and leaves at four he cannot claim to be "value driven".

Prerequisite 2

He has got to be a visionary. He must actively display creative flair and have the ability to look at abstract and non-measurable "things" and make sense of them. This is often difficult for logical, analytical people, but it is possible to cultivate the creative faculty through training.

Prerequisite 3

He must be able to illustrate the courage of his convictions. Anything that is new, contradicts the norm, is controversial, takes courage to talk about let alone implement. He *has* to have the ability to show courage without having access to facts — to be a risk-taker in fact.

Prerequisite 4

He must have energy. The fortunate (or unfortunate) part of implementing a philosophy in which the leader believes, is that he has to get out to his people day and night, from north to south, east to west. He needs the energy to *genuinely* implement the principle of "managing by walking around" — or driving or flying around! If he does not operate with a high degree of visibility, the philosophy will not get off the ground.

Prerequisite 5

He must be dynamic. By dynamism here I mean, able to flow with a changing environment and organisation; bending with the

70

wind without snapping, totally flexible to the environment but not letting up on the philosophy. He has to be able to play a concrete role as a change agent.

Prerequisite 6

He must be communicative. Telling is inflexible, selling is flexible. He needs to be able to "sell" and not be overly concerned with the exactitudes of his communication. A little bit of a politician in the truer sense of the word. If he is too concerned with exactitudes he will be unable to put across his philosophical viewpoint strongly enough.

There are other "nice" qualities to have such as empathy, goal orientation, supportiveness, follow-up, etc. but in the main the preceding six points are prerequisites born out of total commitment. But no matter how brilliant the leader, he can't bring about change and success on his own. The company structure is of great importance.

Towards an organic structure

This was especially true for Cashbuild which operates in a business environment that is basically a fast-changing one. The industry brings in a lot of specialisation in the form of market segmentation and focusing by other businesses. Traditional builders' merchants changed to "cash and carry" overnight to become a competitive force. Changes in business strategies by our opponents forced us to change our strategies. It therefore stands to reason that our form of organisation had to be more differentiating in nature than integrative. So we learned to recognise individual differences in different markets and allow different business units the freedom to "do their own thing". If a branch wanted to offer 50% discounts on merchandise, we didn't ques-

71

tion it. As long as the bottom line results were there. At the same time, you have to at least keep the entire group focusing on the same goals, so there have to be integrative devices for doing this. At Cashbuild, these were the philosophy, the manual, the budgets and team workshops where problems were sorted out face-to-face in an open manner. And thus the ship sailed.

By definition, differentiating means recognising different cognitive as well as emotional values, not only in the market place, but as they concern people. An organisational system had to be conceptualised to cope with this. We needed an organic structure within which there could be a flow of ideas, exchanging of values, constant change and growth, and which would allow instant response to both the internal and external environment. An organic structure would enable us to:

* Recognise that a person in a higher position would not necessarily have a sounder knowledge base than a person at a lower level. The reverse is in fact true when it comes to specific work-related problems. (We soon found this out via VENTURECOMM.)
* Disregard rank and status. No levels should exist if they served only to (de)grade people. Rank and status had to be replaced with *team purpose* and a total commitment to work *together* for common ideals.
* Ensure that no boundaries existed between departments. Problem solving was done through teams which consisted of various departments. Vertical relationships were given less attention than horizontal and lateral cross-company relationships. This made team functioning effective.
* De-emphasise blocks and boxes. Less emphasis was laid on job descriptions and more placed on competence modelling.
* Ensure concern for organisation with wider objectives rather than focusing on sub-speciality. (A greater emphasis to be placed on skill rather than on authority of knowledge).

This organic organisational system would in turn allow us to react to the market place rapidly so that we could ensure that our predominant competitive issue of effectiveness (profitability) was achieved in our dynamic market through participative problem solving.

The management team

As participative problem solving is a soft variable, so effectiveness and profitability are hard variables. The fact of the matter remained that within the context of Cashbuild's shift of emphasis in the soft variable arena, I couldn't do the job of running Cashbuild alone. What with 17 stores to run as well as looking at other developmental areas, it was nigh impossible even to make the philosopy work. I needed a hard variable man. Enter Gerald Haumant.

Gerald was chosen for the specific task of controlling our stores and looking after the effectiveness of their running. He set up an infrastructure of more regional managers and the prosperity of the business improved. Between the two of us, there was the making of a dynamic team. In fact, with hindsight I believe that the CARE plan could never have taken off had it not been for the two specific strengths which we had: vision and risk-taking from me, exceptional follow-up and controlling abilities from him. Whenever I flew too high, he brought me back to earth with his cool, rational thinking and whenever one of his concerns couldn't get moving, I helped him fly a little. Poles apart, but in the eight years of working together I would have chosen it no other way. It was *the* foundation of Cashbuild.

Further support to reinforce commitment to our philosophy was needed in the form of a "people department", which was headed by George Bell. We did not like the word "personnel" so we called it our " people department", because that's what it was. George was chosen to fit in with that framework, not just because of his skill in personnel administration, but for his ability to build up a leadership power base for the "cause". A

73

distinct difference exists here in doing the right things as opposed to doing things right. George is the kind of guy who is willing to travel 6 000 km per month *listening* to what's happening on the floor and selling philosophy and ensuring that the message gets through. Speaking generally, his mission was:

* To win total support from all subordinates
* To guide work patterns in a facilitative manner
* To guide interpersonal and interactive relationships in a facilitative manner
* To ensure that emphasis on goal achievement was maintained.

Without this support function, there would be no leadership in the groups from management and the "cause" could die. An effective communicator like George is a must for strong commitment to the "cause".

An element which distinctly worked in Cashbuild's favour in the implementation of the philosophy, was the fact that it was a new company — no old habits to kill, just perceptions to change. This facilitated the speed of implementation — albeit three years.

Another factor was that we had quite a few managers who were willing to try out alternative solutions and to act as change agents. A couple of ex-Rhodies spring to mind here. Maybe they were more receptive because they'd already been through the trauma of a black/white conflict — be that as it may. In any workforce, there will be people whose energy and enthusiasm can be harnessed. It's a matter of looking for them, wanting to find them.

Now if we bring together the various elements we can say with confidence that the organisational behaviour will be a result of those elements. This is depicted in Figure 11.

Put these together and the organisational behaviour will become dynamic, go-ahead, aggressive and proactive, which in turn will create an exciting and demanding climate in which individuals can excel, achieve *and receive their just reward.*

74

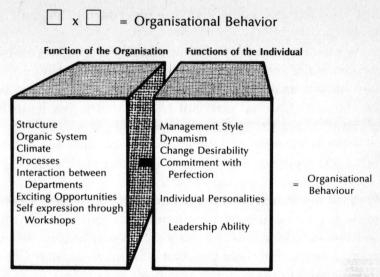

$\square$ x $\square$ = Organisational Behavior

Function of the Organisation **Functions of the Individual**

Structure
Organic System
Climate
Processes
Interaction between
  Departments
Exciting Opportunities
Self expression through
  Workshops

Management Style
Dynamism
Change Desirability
Commitment with
  Perfection

Individual Personalities

Leadership Ability

= Organisational
  Behaviour

Figure 11: Synergy: the impact on organisation and individual

Commitment

It is my deep conviction that other corporations, if *the will* is there, can introduce similar philosophies into their companies without too many headaches — but with a lot of foresight, courage and hard work. Keeping at it relentlessly until it becomes a dream fulfilled, top management has *got to be committed!*

When I talk about commitment, I mean the kind that makes you willing to spend four or five months at a time hardly seeing your family because either you're about to drive off or you're so drained you can't say one more word. I remember, in the early days of VENTURECOMM, we ran into big problems at Potgietersrus. There was a man there who was intimidating the staff. He was a good worker, very competent, the only problem was nobody wanted to be near him in any way. One of the first things the branch VENTURECOMM did was to vote he be fired. So, when he got to hear of it, he called in the union. Nine o'clock one Monday morning, the branch manager telephoned George Bell. By 11.45 that day the Regional Manager was at Potgietersrus, and by 12.15 George was there, on the spot, talking, listening. Exit problem.

We didn't use the telephone for that sort of thing at Cashbuild. In the kind of system we built up, the telephone isn't enough. You have to make contact with a man. You have to know, is he shaking? Can he look you in the eye? Is his handshake clammy?

Another example is our rallies. People ask me how we managed to get our workers to be so enthusiastic about the rallies. The answer is we didn't try to, because we didn't have to. Because top management was always there, with the people, talking. When you do that, you build up your own hero-base, so when people see there's going to be a rally next month, they want to be there to hear you. But it was our commitment that took us among them in the first place.

Cashbuild and luck

Has the CARE plan actually worked? This is normally where the faint-hearted and logical rationalists get off. When we tell them that our results are *because* of *team and people* effort, they say "no way — you were lucky".

Lucky? How can you be "lucky" in a recession, the worst since the Great Depression? How can you be "lucky" in the third worst-hit sector of the economy? With all the political unrest and turbulence going on in an unstable environment and economy? How can you call it "luck" when your stores increase from 17 to 26 (53%) over a three-year period but profit before tax jumps from R600 000 to R3,8 million (533%) over the same period?

At a problem store (Pietersburg) with sales of R35 000 per week, a customer focus evening revealed that customers were constantly being told that things were out of stock. Our actual in-store shopping list revealed 86% in stock on Top 100 lines. The

CARE group brainstormed the problem, a bonus system was introduced and six months later the situation was tested at another customer focus evening. "Stock levels are fantastic", our customers told us. However the internal shopping list again revealed 85% in stock. No difference in *actual* stock levels but a change in perception. Sales jumped to R100 000 per week and remained there. Was this luck? Or had the caddies been saying "sorry we're out of stock" simply because they actually weren't committed to the business at the time? It's amazing how, suddenly, sales caddies "found" stock once they were paid a participative bonus.

Is it luck that a staff member who catches a customer stealing is, nowadays, willing to report it, perhaps at the risk of his own life? We know it helps reduce shrinkage, which is straight off the bottom line — and so does he!

Is it luck that your VENTURECOMM members write a report on an inadequate branch manager whom you have to fire? In the ivory tower you don't see these things, but thank God, other committed soldiers are helping to run your business.

No sir, it is *not* luck. *Team is **everything.*** To the sceptics I say: Go ahead, sit back with the excuse that the government is at fault and that they must make the first move.

Go ahead, hide behind the fact that in your organisation good industrial relations is something beyond your personal control.

If you say "the government must make the first move", you're going to find out that it's too late.

If you say "good industrial relations is beyond your personal control", you're going to *have to* find out that union men are "nice" people.

If you say "my people are lazy and unproductive" you're going to find that they are in fact so and you're not going to wonder what happened to your productivity figures.

In every instance as a "business" man you will be to blame for any misfortune coming your way, unless you are willing to change your traditional South African view, be proactive and play an active role in helping to create a better South African environment. It is your moral obligation as a capitalist and businessman.

Surviving

The driving force at Cashbuild was survival. In South Africa we are currently going through some traumatic changes at the macro level and business as we know it today will no doubt take on another form in the future. What we have done is to put our business in a position to cope with any changes which come our way in the South Africa of tomorrow. Our obligation to prepare our employees for future change has been of paramount importance and formed an integral part of our organisational development.

 We sincerely believe that a new breed of manager is needed in South Africa. A manager who loses the title "boss" but acquires the new label of leader. A manager who approaches the future, not with scepticism and fear, but with insight, sensitivity and vision. Only in this manner can we build toward a better South Africa.

9/2

*The bravest thing you can do when you are not brave is to profess courage and **act** accordingly* (Dr Wayne Dyer)

10 Fear of failure — the death knell of participation

sound of bell
of a funeral

In our society we have come to learn that success is the only acceptable standard to live by and that to experiment with the unknown (new ways of doing things) is taboo. The contrary holds more truth — nothing fails like success because we do not learn anything from it. Without failure we can learn nothing. Yes, success does breed success and we readily pursue success but actually we learn nothing new. This is the dilemma of change.

If Einstein, Galileo, Beethoven, Da Vinci, Churchill, Edison, Columbus and a host of other pioneers of yesteryear avoided the unknown, we as a society would not have benefited from their adventures into the new and untried. They were all people, just like us, set apart only in that they were willing to traverse areas where others dared not tread. Their greatness is generally only discernible in the *quality of exploration* and the boldness with which they explored the unknown.

Our current society has unfortunately developed far too many risk-averse individuals who have become safety experts, that is, individuals who shun the unknown in favour of always having to know where they're going and what they can expect when they get there. Early training in our society has tended to encourage caution at the expense of curiosity, safety at the expense of adventure. However, the unknown is the source of all growth and excitement.

You can never be prepared for the unknown. That is a contradiction in terms. Could you imagine a mother saying to a child "Don't stand up on your feet until you've learned to walk"? It is actually this ridiculousness which causes us to develop "programmes" for Black Advancement, Worker Participation and Equal Employment Opportunities. We believe that by developing programmes in this manner we will be in a position to look at all angles and obstacles which we may encounter in future and then we will be sufficiently prepared to overcome them. The truth of the matter is, however, that we can only cope with the unknown, or the future, or change, by *experiencing* it and acting on alternatives as and when they arise. We can never learn by just thinking of future obstacles. Doing is the antidote of fear because we can never know what it feels like to get rid of fear until we confront it and experiment with life itself.

We simply have to get out there, fumble around, fail a lot, try this and change that and then question whether this will actually decrease our wisdom and chances of success or enhance growth and prosperity. If we continue to refuse to give ourselves over to life's experiences, we are actually saying that we "choose to refuse to know and understand", and by refusing to understand we are assured of falling victim to immobilisation and the eventual demise of our organisation. The old way simply will not cope with the "new" order in South Africa.

Participation paralysis

The breakaway from the old way is not easy. It takes courage. Courage is nothing else but the *willingness to confront fear*. Courage means flying in the face of criticism and the willingness to accept and learn from the consequences of all our choices.

On many occasions it has been asked of participative management "What about the loss of control? What if the plan fails? What about our power bases — our right to control?" These questions all stem from fear of the unknown, but the paradox is that there is no such thing as fear. Fear simply does not exist in the world. Fear is what we do to ourselves by *thinking* fearful thoughts and having fearsome *expectations*. Fear is born from some preconceived notion of expected outcomes and even though they are not provable, we prefer to retreat into *avoidance behaviour*. This immobilises us and we would rather say "fascinating, participation can work for him, but for us ... no way".

In order to understand this paralysis we need to probe a little further into why organisations behave in this manner.

The unknown confronts us and this means change. From preconceived notions of expected (unreal) outcomes we feel threatened and in turn this causes tension and stress. Because of this stress and tension we become immobilised because we are unable to "plan" outcomes or "be prepared" for the unknown. Growth is further impeded because of our avoidance behaviour which then produces a self-fulfilling prophecy.

There are many cultural reasons for this and these are explained below.

Organisational rigidity — Taylorism

There are many people in high places who find it difficult to be spontaneous. Every morning at 07h00 these executives take the freeway. They plan every day to the minute. The coffee comes at exactly 10h00. The secretary takes dictation at 11h00. They rigidly hang on to their accustomed behaviours. They try nothing new or out of line or, if it is new it is yet another bureaucratic system which affirms success or control. They are oblivious to the absurdities which they blindly follow. They are victims of the system. Executives who speak spontaneously at board meetings are often ex-executives shortly afterwards. But many executives desperately fear the unknown. They fit in. They do what they are told. They never challenge but rigidly adhere to what is expected of them. They tend to do things the way they have always been done; they never grow because "success" has already been achieved. Success at the expense of creative life. Success at the cost of living moment by moment in a sponaneous manner. Joy eludes them.

Their organisations are designed the same way — mechanistic and rigid because everything must be predictable. They programme everything and box anything they can find. They effectively annihilate the human spirit. Have they really been developing their jobs for 20 years or have they been doing their job every year, twenty times over? If only they could understand that spontaneity and openness bring out the best in the human spirit and make life exciting, something they could enjoy. Spontaneity brings communication and understanding that can open all the doors to better results in the organisation.

Prejudice and the "old way"

Prejudice is based less on hate or even dislike of people, ideas and activities, than on the fact that it is easier and safer to stay with the known. That is, people who are like you and think the same as you do. Gradually, although prejudices feel comfortable, they work against you because they prevent you from exploring the unknown. They keep you safe from encountering murky and fuzzy elements, such as normal human behaviour and puzzling provinces of the unknown, and they actually prevent growth or coping with change.

The "old way" says that we must control human beings by boxing them because we can't trust them in our endeavours. By saying we don't trust anyone unless we can get a "handle" on them, what we actually mean is that we can't trust ourselves even on familiar ground — we are insecure.

Prejudice brings insecurity which immobilises us in interacting with people of other values. We simply must become more spontaneous on an interactive communication basis if we want to shed prejudice.

mental disturbance

Success neurosis and communication

Fear of failure is a powerful fear in our society, one which has been inculcated in our childhood and after, and carried through life. Failure is simply the system's opinion of how a certain action should have been completed in order to "comply with certain standards or norms". So in our organisations, we now overlay preconceived notions of how not to fail, and then design programmes and boxes to "prevent" failure. If we do "fail", then we take the failure upon ourselves as people and this eventually gets in the way of innovation and experimentation. If people in an organisation communicate (talk with each other not at each other) on a daily basis, many pitfalls will be avoided as the *experience of doing* not *the plan of prescription* takes place.

A lion roars. Can we grade the quality of his roar as an A, B or C roar? It is impossible for the lion to fail at roaring because there is no *provision* for evaluating his roar. Lions hunt buck, if they are not successful in catching one they simply try again. They don't lie there and whine complaining about the one that got away, or have a nervous breakdown because they failed.

To us humans, communication is natural — but we put obstacles in our way that stop us communicating. We actually "grade" communication and prevent people from talking to one another — either through prejudice or because of rigid hierarchies. What would originally have been a natural process — for the boss to communicate directly with workers at any level — becomes unnatural by virtue of structures which *should not have existed in the first place.* Our fear is therefore unfounded because by <u>communicating</u> all we are doing is what comes naturally to us — to everyone's advantage.

Here in South Africa, we are particularly scared of talking to one another, in all kinds of situations, not just on a national, political level. A man who is unhappily married, for instance, won't talk about it to his wife, or his best friend, because he's afraid of talking. So he stays unhappy in his marriage. At Cashbuild we have attacked that fear with a vengeance. At the end of a workshop, I would often invite a few people to join me for dinner, and I'd ask them to bring their wives along. That in itself was often a breakthrough in getting people to talk to one another — in a place like Pietersburg blacks and whites don't go out to restaurants together! On one occasion, I found myself having supper with three extreme right-wing whites, and three very radical black men from the Cape. By the end of our three-hour meal, no-one was talking about the Hippos in the townships anymore, or who was killing whose children. We were discussing how we could modify people's working hours so that when they came to work during an extended stay-away, their absence from the townships wouldn't be so visible. Now, if you're afraid of communicating, you won't ever be able to solve that kind of problem.

Organisational security — the right to control

Security means knowing what's going to happen. Security means no growth. Security means no excitement, no risks, and no challenges. Everything in our lives is pre-planned like an essay — introduction, a well-organised body, and a conclusion. This type of life and thinking keep us from living in the present moment. Living according to the plan implies a guarantee that everything will be OK forever.

We normally measure security in the form of possessions such as money, a house, a job, a business or a position in the community. If we are now "in charge" of these things, we believe we have control over our destiny and if some "intruder" shares it with us we will lose our "control". This fear of loss of control is immense and is born from our western standards of individualism. Typically, in a business, individuality breeds selfishness and in time selfishness breeds greed and we find it much easier to "control" people (in boxes). Our position must remain unchallenged because we have a "vested" interest. What we forget is that if we were to go into battle we would need every soldier to help protect us against a common onslaught, otherwise even we as bosses or leaders would perish. However, when the time comes for the organisation to go into battle as a single entity, individuals are not "free" to defend the status quo. Our own selfishness in allowing people "too little say" in the organisation becomes our own worst enemy at the time of an onslaught against the organisation.

I have never heard of a General lose a particular battle when he allows his scouts in the front lines to give him feedback on enemy strengths.

Some strategies for coming to grips with fear of participation

Before we can come to grips with some simple strategies for overcoming the fear of participation, we must first understand the positive cycle of change confrontation.

The unknown confronts us and this means change. From preconceived notions of expected (unreal) outcomes, we can become threatened. But we should see change as an opportunity for growth. This means risk, innovation and creativity and the mustering of courage to act with the right motivation.

We can see, therefore, that from doing and experiencing we start understanding, which in turn places us in a position of strength and confidence to carry on. Once understanding is at hand uncharted waters will no longer be feared because we will be sailing in them.

Strategy 1
Spiders construct webs - not successful or unsuccessful ones. The web in organisation is communication. The communication web can easily be established simply by changing from ''tell'' type staff meetings to meaningful probe and question type meetings, exploring all facets of the business. No hidden agendas but totally exploratory with no right or wrong way of doing it.

Strategy 2
Instead of individuals being given the task of finding solutions to problems, appoint teams to probe the factors around the problem and report with action plans and possible solutions to the problem. This could take place throughout the organisation at all levels.

Strategy 3
Look for pockets in the organisation which lend themselves to total participation and start there. Don't be too concerned about chains of communication and position of individuals, let it flow.

Strategy 4
Think through a plan for participation, but *don't* develop a programme. First you think, second you *do* and only third will you know and understand what to do next and how to proceed further.

None of the above is threatening or disruptive to an organisation. It is only with time that new strategies will have to be developed to cope with new changes as and when they arise.

Never in Cashbuild did we ever envisage what would happen when we started talking to our people. Scepticism was there, yes, but through simple communication in the first two years, we managed to build up an arsenal of defences against the fear of failure. The rest is history.

Last word

To conclude, we can only mention that Cashbuild has done everything in its power to cope with the changing South African environment and the changing demands stemming from that environment. We believe that we have sincerely contributed, albeit in a small way, to our greater macro environment in terms of closing the cultural gap. Of this we are proud and we believe that every one of our employees feels the same way as well. If they didn't we don't believe that we could have achieved the results which have made for so much success over the last three years. It's the *team* which made our company successful and it's the *team* which, we know, will win the future.

Our greatest resource at Cashbuild is our people, and we believe that our caring organisation has created an unbelievably trusting atmosphere in which human beings feel motivated and can develop their full potential. I see it as part of our obligation to our fellow man, black as well as white.

Often we have been criticised by others in industry as being ''soft'', as ''interfering with politics'', as being ''leftist''. We've even been threatened by extremists. We are not moved by these criticisms and accusations because the only thing that we're guilty of is giving genuine freedom to our employees at their place of work.

The need for the individual to feel free and to give expression to his freedom has been a major need throughout history. Freedom moulds the future and turns human beings on. In turn they, as workers, produce more profit and it is this profit that gives us the freedom we are looking for. We have been no less capitalistic than that.

One last word. I want to leave you with a likely picture of the average South African man ten years from now.

He is black.
He is 18 years old.
He has either witnessed or taken part in an act of violence.
He is literate — but only just.
He has no father.
He has no work.

Quo vadis, Mr South African Manager?

9|2·

PART TWO

Nasser
Nel

Introduction

The ensuing chapters are intended to critique the whole Cashbuild story and its broader application to business in the South African context. More importantly the authors are attempting to examine the universality of these concepts. It is with much enthusiasm therefore that the remaining chapters are devoted to a critical review of what can be learnt from the Cashbuild story.

What distinguishes leaders from managers according to Zaleznik (1977) is their ability to be visionary and proactive. Visionary leadership within the context of creating employee commitment, implies an ability to release pent-up energies for the good of organisational efficiency. It implies that the leader will take a stance of risk. Creativity and initiative will therefore become the order of the day and far from being risk-averse, the corporation will allow for its employees to focus their energies in new directions. One of the fundamental issues will be that of creating an environment in which entrepreneurship and all that this implies is alive and well and that employees are able to benefit from their involvement in such entrepreneurial activity. According to Clive Weil from the Checkers group, profit is the product of a vote of confidence in management from its employees.

The focus in visionary management is towards liberating the latent, pent-up energies in the direction of achieving the corporate cause, thereby generating greater wealth creation. Whether this reflects itself in a management style which propounds "Sharing the Loot" or "Power to the People" or "A Rewards based Culture", the impact is much the same. The corporate army is marching towards winning the competitor war and creating the kind of organisational leadership which makes for the best possible return-on-assets.

91

11
The organisational crisis

That people are the major generators of profit cannot be disputed. From such eminent authors as Bennis (1985), Porter (1986), Argyris (1970), Athos (1983), Schein (1984), Robey (1980), Zaleznik (1977) and Drucker (1985) has come a flood of publications all confirming the central role of people in organisational effectiveness. Indeed, this realisation is nothing new; it is as old as the first enterprise whose accomplishment depended upon the joint effort of a group of people and their leader. Yet the issue of gaining employee commitment remains unresolved in the majority of business enterprises. By its nature, this is a variable over which management cannot gain ultimate control. At best, management can only attempt to create the kind of corporate environment which will enthuse people about the organisation they work for.

The standard concepts of planning, leading, organising, controlling (PLOC), which have been regarded as the four commandments of management, apparently chiselled on tablets of stone, have been inadequate to resolve the problem of employee commitment. It seems that PLOC management ensures that minimum standards are met - a mediocre kind of outcome at the best of times, and quite unacceptable for any organisation striving for excellence or confronted by extraordinary challenges from the macro environment. PLOC management, with its characteristically mechanistic approach, is unable to develop a corporate environment which can cater for people's specific needs, accommodate their unique natures, and provide them with a sense of dignity and belonging; and it is precisely this type of environment which breeds committed people, without whom the challenges of excellence or, in the case of South Africa, survival itself, cannot be met.

Employee perceptions: the key to corporate commitment

The way in which individual employees interact with the corporate environment determines whether the employee's perception of the corporation is negative or positive (Nasser, 1986). This in turn influences his behaviour to a marked degree. Negative perceptions may generate behaviours that are counterproductive and, in extreme cases, may be part of the motivation that prompts acts of industrial sabotage. *—ve perceps.*

Positive perceptions, on the other hand, engender enthusiasm and a commitment to corporate objectives. A person who views the corporation positively will make every possible effort to achieve those objectives. *+ve preceps.*

Clearly, management should endeavour to elicit positive perceptions in order to achieve the best return on its human resource asset. *cl*

The corporate environment: the key to employee perceptions

An organisation can influence, but not finally determine, how an individual perceives his environment. What the organisation *can* determine is the nature of the corporate environment that the employee perceives, and into which he must immerse himself, with all his needs, goals, dreams and hopes. Figure 12 depicts the ideal of an exact fit between the individual and the corporate environment (Nasser, 1986). *note*

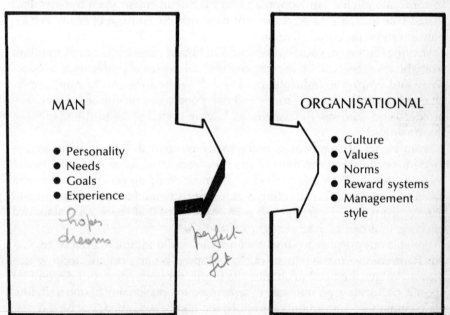

Figure 12: Management/Organisation fit

93

A highly mechanistic organisation, with its adherence to a rigid structure and functional regimentation, is unlikely to be able to provide a culture in which the individual can meet more than his basic needs. Negative perceptions will emerge from a corporate environment such as this, from which are likely to arise high levels of frustration. Organisations with a more organic structure which is flexible enough to afford a more comfortable niche for the individual worker as a whole human being, are most likely to optimise employee commitment. The importance of healthy corporate environments can therefore never be underestimated because the individual is both the instrument and the result of corporate behaviour.

Transforming the corporate environment

Corporate cultures which recognise people as the major actors in making organisations effective are the winners for both the present and future. The last decade has seen an increasing movement towards participative management throughout the developed world, for this very reason. Both Peters and Waterman (1982) and Peters and Austin (1985) have indicated in their examination of excellent corporations that involvement in whatever shape and form is a key component in commitment and hence corporate success. The story of Cashbuild is the story of how one company achieved participation in corporate affairs. For Koopman and his management team the essential thrust was to create an environment in which the concept of employee involvement could come alive.

The question is, of course, how did Cashbuild achieve its transformation from the average, PLOC-style company with all the usual problems of productivity and employee indifference? How did it become the vibrant, supercharged organisation it is today, whose people are proud of being Cashbuilders and who see themselves as having a vital stake in the success of the business?

From Part 1 of this book it will already be clear that there is no ready-made formula along the lines of the PLOC recipe for achieving this kind of transformation. The gurus of the management world agree; and readers who are acquainted with outstanding organisations noted for their cohesion and team spirit will know from their own experience that there is no standard package that can be had straight off the shelf.

Yet, it is our purpose to show that the Cashbuild experience *can* be repeated. Participative management *can* be adopted by any organisation which acknowledges the need to change. Its implementation does not depend on specific circumstances, nor does it depend on the personality of one individual. Koopman's achievements cannot be too highly acclaimed; but he did not, in fact, perform a miracle. He followed a number of well-known and well-tried principles (whether by intent or through his own discovery), which

94

may be identified and followed by anyone else. A further point of note is that Koopman followed *all* the principles whereby participative management may be implemented and kept in place as the essential characteristic of the organisation. Other organisations which have experimented with participative management - and failed - have not, in fact, gone all the way, but have tried out this and that, changed a system or two, tinkered around with the organisation chart.

The philosophy which underlies the movement towards worker participation is developed and explored in the chapters that follow. The core issues of this philosophy are briefly presented below:

* A new way of thinking has to be developed. The cause-and-effect approach, which produces quick-fix solutions and encourages reactivity, must be supplanted by a long-term, holistic view of the organisation as a dynamic *process*.
* Management commitment to the transformation, all the way down the line, is vital. Top management's commitment will provide the driving inspiration, while committed line managers will actually implement the transformation act by act.
* Participation must become the central focus of the business plan. Marketing strategies, capital expenditure policies, technological advances - all these are secondary since they will be shaped by the transformation.
* Leadership and vision have to be developed to replace sterile managing and planning activities.
* The corporate environment must be prepared. Unless workers have reason to believe that management are acting in good faith, they are unlikely to cooperate. In Cashbuild, this was achieved through the process of value trading.
* The organisation's culture and structure will have to be adapted to the new philosophy. This is usually a gradual process taking place over a period of years rather than weeks.
* Open communication, unhampered by status, rigid procedures or role norms, must be institutionalised.
* Acknowledgement of the dignity of the worker as a human being and of his or her right to justice in the workplace are at the heart of the philosophy of worker participation. These beliefs must be established as realities within the organisation.
* Reward systems must be devised which will operate in accordance with the philosophy.
* The system should be personalised to suit the company as a unique entity.

95

In keeping with this last issue, we wish to emphasise yet again that these core issues cannot be assembled into a package. Participative management will not become a reality in any organisation unless all these issues are taken into account; yet for each organisation there is a unique combination or sequence or emphasis which must be discovered. The introduction of worker participation is a risky business; there is no "safe" route to transformation and excellence.

Towards excellence

In looking for the extra mile as described in the Cashbuild philosophy the maximum devolution of power was a key issue. The formulation of the CARE groups and VENTURECOMM was intended to facilitate this devolution of power and so create the greatest sense of employee and corporate commitment. Excellence in this context implies that newer and better ways of optimising business opportunities come from a liberated workforce.

In describing the whole field of entrepreneurship, Drucker points out the critical issue of liberating employee minds. This means that the fundamentals of creativity, innovation and risk-taking can only come from employees who believe they are free to test new ideas, find new solutions, open new markets, and construct and reconstruct management thinking in terms of the demands of the business at that particular point in time. Creativity is rewarded in such environments and corporate value systems make organisational heroes of people who are creative in the workplace. Individual commitment is the key issue here, and is often the product of a sense of belonging to the greater corporate family.

Management can only create ideal working environments such as that of Cashbuild when it is in constant touch with what is happening on the shop floor. The structuring and restructuring of the corporate environment has to be the result of management's constant assessment of where the corporation is heading at any one time. The discovery of the MBFA (Management by Fumbling Around) concept in Cashbuild was the outcome of such ongoing assessments. In striving to create an environment of trust which would advance corporate interest, Koopman discovered that the most critical issue was constant interaction with the people on the shop floor.

In Koopman's philosophy this sense of belonging to a greater corporate family, and the human dignity which accompanies it, are fundamental to the success of the business. Committed soldiers who are on the battle front fighting the war have more than just a fundamental understanding of the battle and its objectives. They have become part of the process in creating the strategy which will win the battle. They are committed soldiers because they understand not only the direction but also the process of the battle.

96

Questions such as: will the process work in a bigger organisation? can it work in sectors such as mining and finance? are the chances of success in a decentralised business as good as those in a centralised system? have to be answered to determine the extent to which Koopman's philosophy can be applied across the broader spectrum of South African business.

9/2.

12
The transformation

A given organisation will usually only embark on the voyage to transformation once it is confronted by problems that signal the need for far-reaching changes. Cashbuild's revolutionary organisational structure and management style were born from a recognition of the need to change and develop new strategies in order to address the crisis that was facing the organisation. In Albert Koopman's words: ''Our profits were on the rise up to 1982 then suddenly they dipped. Ostensibly at that stage there was a boom, but we weren't seeing any of its benefits. We blamed it on opening too many new stores in one year but that wasn't the real reason. I wasn't happy with that. So I decided to dedicate one year of research into the reason for our business not going the way it was supposed to. I conducted four workshops across the country with my managers, and I asked them exactly what they would like to see. What was their perception of Cashbuild as a company? Where did they believe Cashbuild would go as a business? How did it fit into the whole South African scenario? How could we best satisfy the needs of our employees and turn them on in working for our common objective — corporate profit?''

The basis of Cashbuild's successful transformation is reflected in these words. The Cashbuild management were not willing to implement *ad hoc* or incremental changes to try to cope with the dilemma that was facing them. They realised that a new strategy had to be based on thorough research which involved ascertaining the opinions and ideas of all the managers in the system. Workers were also later involved, which ensured that all employees at Cashbuild felt part of the transformation that was occurring. Cashbuild's willingness to allow its employees to participate in the reshaping of the organisation was a key element in the success of the transformation process.

A further element was the acknowledgement of the external factors that demanded basic shifts in the way the company was operating. New legislation, social tensions, world instability, unforeseen competition, escalating costs, material shortages, were all external factors that would create new threats and opportunities for an organisation. A strategy that takes cognisance of micro or internal issues only will not succeed because it will not cope effectively with the macro scenario within which the business has to operate.

There can be but a handful of South African managers who would deny that the social and political tensions of our particular macro environment present a grave threat, not just to individual companies, but to the very substance of the free enterprise system. Few would quarrel with the view that if South African companies do not themselves initiate the process of transformation, they will be faced with a transformation imposed upon them by external forces.

Yet let it be said that South African business is not alone in facing the kind of challenge that demands an entirely new adaptation to a radically changing environment. The urgency with which American corporations are examining their systems, cultures and philosophies is indicative of the extent to which they are being threatened by the Japanese. It is ruefully accepted by the Americans that Japanese workers are committed to their organisations in a way that few American corporations can boast of.

Once a company has taken the decision to ensure it survives the internal and external threats it faces by implementing a philosphy of worker participation, it must begin taking action for the decision to become a reality. The initial steps taken by Cashbuild are pinpointed below and discussed in some detail.

MBWA and MBFA

The concepts of MBWA (Management by Walking Around) and MBFA (Management by Fumbling Around) have become part of management life in the Cashbuild organisation. The Cashbuild management recognised early on the need to find unique solutions to its particular problems. The standard autocratic and rigidly controlling management of the past had not delivered the answers. The alternative was to go the route of discovery in creating new solutions for old problems. MBFA was the name Cashbuild gave to this process. Management realised that it would have to live with the discomforts of fumbling around and understood that this exploratory process required a great deal of faith and willingness to take risks. The success of MBFA depends on how much MBWA is done. The fumbling around process is not confined to the boardroom but through consistent participation and negotiation takes place at all levels of the organisation. The formulation of strategy and direction is therefore based on management's awareness of needs and feelings at the operational level, which plays a major role in the successful execution of any strategy.

Changing perceptions - a core issue towards transformation

One of the first conclusions that Albert Koopman reached in his research into the causes of Cashbuild's crisis was that there was a lack of cohesion in the company. Managers felt that the company was viable, it had a sound structure, and all the necessary controls for success seemed to be in place. But brainstorming pointed with alarming consistency to a lack of motivation among black staff. According to managers, workers at the operational level did not seem to care for the company. They didn't understand the business, were badly educated, did not seem to take well to training, did not want to talk sufficiently and openly to managers and generally did not seem really interested in productivity or high levels of quality. The major problem, it would seem, was incongruence between the management's and workers' perceptions of the business.

Koopman's comment on the negative perceptions was: "How on God's earth were we going to win the war if we had soldiers who didn't even understand or know the enemy?"

The conclusions reached were directly in line with the findings of the nationally approved "Project Free Enterprise" (Nasser, 1987). The perceptions of workers with regard to business and its impact upon them are best reflected in Figure 13.

Peters and Watermann (1982) point out that productivity through people is one of the eight key principles to success in creating corporate excellence. A positive attitude towards the business and its objectives is fundamental to creating the best effort from the human resources within the organisation.

The crucial issues surrounding the interpretation of Figure 13 are reflected in the following:

* The perceptions reflect a high level of resistance towards business and the free market system which are perceived as being exploitative by nature. This pertains also to the broader socioeconomic and sociopolitical environment.
* The free market system is perceived as having very little benefit for the worker, and is believed to be mainly conducted for the benefit of (white) management who are also viewed as being the owners of the business.
* The perceptions reflect a feeling that the outputs and benefits of business have very little direct benefit for the worker as supplier of the labour inputs. For this reason there is very little motivation for the worker to improve his labour inputs since it is believed that this would really only

100

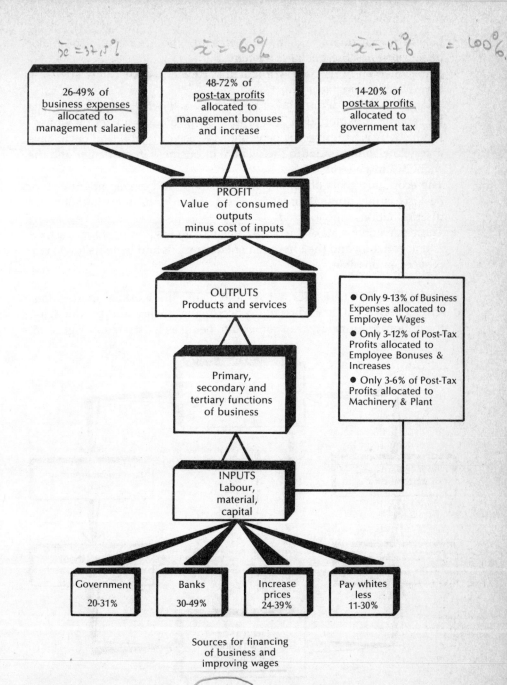

$\bar{x} = 37.5\%$ $\bar{x} = 60\%$ $\bar{x} = 17\%$ $= 60\%$

26-49% of
business expenses
allocated to
management salaries

48-72% of
post-tax profits
allocated to
management bonuses
and increase

14-20% of
post-tax profits
allocated to
government tax

PROFIT
Value of consumed
outputs
minus cost of inputs

OUTPUTS
Products and services

● Only 9-13% of Business
Expenses allocated to
Employee Wages

● Only 3-12% of Post-Tax
Profits allocated to
Employee Bonuses &
Increases

● Only 3-6% of Post-Tax
Profits allocated to
Machinery & Plant

Primary,
secondary and
tertiary functions
of business

INPUTS
Labour,
material,
capital

Government
20-31%

Banks
30-49%

Increase
prices
24-39%

Pay whites
less
11-30%

Sources for financing
of business and
improving wages

Figure 13: Workers' linear perception of business

PERCEPTION PROBLEM.   101

benefit management and the government who are already the major beneficiaries of the business system.

* Semiskilled and unskilled workers in particular feel that they are being severly discriminated against.
* The vast majority of the worker group are black, which creates a definite perception of exploitation and repression of black workers by whites.
* Productivity is hampered by perceptions which cause the workers to have a very low commitment to the welfare of business in particular and the economy in general.
* The economic goals of stability, productivity and development cannot be successfully pursued unless workers' perceptions of exploitation and discrimination are corrected.
* These perceptions make the development of an environment for constructive negotiation and the improvement of rewards and benefits for all employees impossible.

Project Free Enterprise further indicated that the workers' perceptions described above will lead directly to decreasing quality and productivity. A perception-productivity trap comes into being as illustrated in Figure 14.

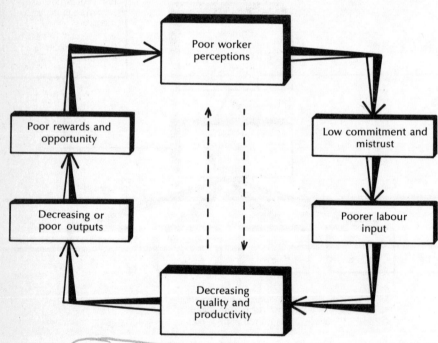

Figure 14: Perception-productivity trap

102

It is clear that the workforce will not commit itself to enhancing quality and productivity whilst negative perceptions prevail. The failure of business to address the real causes of these perceptions will create a situation whereby quality and productivity can only be attained through more and more mechanisation of the business processes. Such short-term thinking will of necessity create increasing unemployment and decreasing job opportunities for the majority of the working population. This will in turn merely reinforce the already prevailing negative perceptions. It is therefore disturbing that many businesses are not focusing sufficient attention on resolving the causes of these perceptions.

Koopman's decision to focus his energy on changing the perceptions of his workforce by integrating all staff into the functioning of the business through participation, right to the floor sweeper, was therefore not only an altruistic or idealistic idea but also, perhaps, a recognition that this is the only way real change and transformation can be effected in the South African business environment.

Creating a more flexible structure

High structure and the mechanistic approach that goes with such a structure were actually detrimental to the Cashbuild business. Transformation depends on flexibility and holism. It was therefore imperative that this highly structured approach be replaced by something that was far more fluid and integrative.

Bennis in his *Temporary Society* and Tofler in *Future Shock* both identified the need for adhocracy rather than bureaucracy as a way of corporate life. In rapidly changing times, they argued, bureaucracy is not enough. By bureaucracy they meant the formal organisational structure that has been established to deal with the routine, everyday items of business - sales, manufacturing, and so on. By adhocracy they meant organisational mechanisms that deal with all the new issues that either fall between bureaucratic cracks or span so many levels that it is not clear who should do what; consequently, in a bureaucracy, nobody does anything.

The concept of organisational fluidity therefore is not new. Certainly, the excellent companies seem to know how to make good use of it. Whether by means of their informal communications networks, or their special ways of using *ad hoc* devices such as task forces, the excellent companies get quick action just because their organisations are fluid.

MBFA is essentially a type of adhocracy. Koopman's aim was for his people to understand the Cashbuild business and to contribute to it in all its facets - so that ultimately they would become more involved and thus more productive. MBFA was a vital strategy in breaking down Cashbuild's tight structure in order to bring about a far more fluid organisation. This is in

103

essence a bias for action. It is furthermore a fostering of a climate where dedication to the central values of the company is the order of the day. Koopman's new structure was in line with the corporate philosophy of involving people in all facets of the business. It led to the creation of a pyramid with five key elements: customer, the employee, company, the competitor/supplier, and motivation/the extra mile.

Integrating staff into the business through participation

Executives generally agree that a freeing of the corporate environment is highly conducive to creating employee enthusiasm and ultimate commitment, and this thinking is generally reflected in corporate policy statements. Unfortunately this is where it ends. As the message makes its way down the many levels of the organisational hierarchy, it seems to become filtered, to grow thinner and thinner as it goes lower down the organisational levels. There often appears to be an unwillingness on the part of managers and supervisors lower down in the organisation to implement the thinking of the policy makers. What is also noticeable is that as one moves down the hierarchical ladder in such organisations, perceptions towards the organisation and its objectives tend to become more negative.

The complacency at senior managerial levels, combined with resistance to change at middle-managerial and supervisory levels, threaten to reinforce workers' perceptions that they are exploited by business. This creates the very real risk that management will increasingly be viewed as merely paying lip-service to full economic participation whilst effectively maintaining the status quo.

Cashbuild's experience in the early days of its change to participation provides a vivid example of the problems that arise when employees are either not convinced by top management's commitment or are opposed to it. To start with, workers withheld their cooperation from the Presidents; and some branch managers paid lip-service to the new philosophy. The point is not, however, that Cashbuild failed to achieve a thorough-going commitment at the outset, but that top management very soon *knew* about the problem and took steps to correct the situation. Further, they repeatedly read the corporate temperature, as it were, by testing and analysing attitudes and through adopting MBWA and MBFA as habitual, characteristic ways of operating. This became part of the process - not just of transformation, but of the organisation itself.

The impact on quality and productivity

As illustrated in Figure 13 the workforce perceives business as a linear process which offers no substantial benefits for the worker. Ideally busi-

104

ness should be viewed as a cyclic process which is driven by an integrated philosophy in which the goals of quality and productivity are of central importance.

Figure 15 shows this cyclic process of business as an integration of the essential components of an organisation, namely the supplier, the customer,

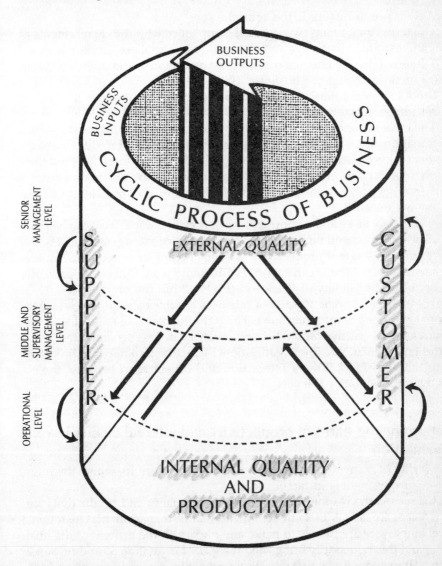

Figure 15: Integrated process of business in excellent companies

quality and productivity. All levels of responsibility revolve around these components. The following may also be noted:

* Free enterprise is seen as a wealth-generating process in which the inputs of a business primarily finance the gains of the output of that business.
* Adherence to quality is the central issue.
  * External quality has two aspects: compliance with the requirements of the external customers and the quality of suppliers' performance.
  * Internal quality ensures the effective operation of the interdependent functions within the business itself.
* Productivity is internally focused ensuring that optimum utilisation of resources is made.
* The locus of control shifts from level to level within the organisation. External quality is the major responsibility of senior and middle management whilst the lower levels of the organisation need to understand their own role in delivering a high level of quality for the external customer.

  Internal quality is the combined responsibility of all individuals within the organisation.

  The daily tasks and responsibilities of the operational level can be more clearly defined and monitored than at the senior management levels and for this reason real productivity can only be implemented at the operational levels of the organisation. Productivity would therefore primarily be the responsibility of the lower levels within the organisation.

This integrated cyclic process of business assumes a vast network of informal and open communications. The right people have to be able to talk to one another openly without becoming bogged down in complicated procedures and regulations. The organisational structure also needs to be simple and lean allowing a flow of interaction and consultation between the executive and operational levels.

Determine the status of productivity and internal quality in your organisation

The reality of many organisations is depicted in Figure 16, where the internal quality triangle is in fact inverted.

This means the responsibilities for internal quality and productivity improvement are held entirely by senior and middle management. Operational level employees are unable to make any impact on the process of the business, and this necessarily brings about a lack of commitment and responsibility. This situation also prevents management from exercising any real control over external quality as it is too busy performing operational functions.

To determine the shape of your internal quality triangle you could use the following questions as a guideline:

* From which levels of responsibility do suggestions continuously come? (Operational/Middle/Senior)

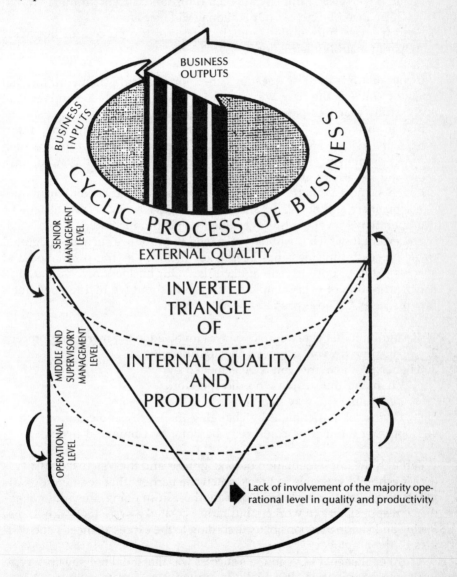

Figure 16: Inverted "internal quality triangle"

* At which levels are decisions generally made? (Operational/Middle/Senior)
* Which levels are always involved in decision-making? (Operational/Middle/Senior)
* Which levels clearly understand their future and current productivity and performance objectives? (Operational/Middle/Senior)
* Which levels fully understand the basics of the process of business? (Operational/Middle/Senior)

If your answers to these questions are : "operational" then your internal quality triangle is the right way up and yours is probably a company that successfully practises participative management.

If your answers are "middle to senior" then you have an inverted internal quality triangle and you will probably be experiencing symptoms such as low productivity, high waste, high shrinkage, lack of worker commitment and negativity at operational levels.

It must be noted that the shape of the triangle is also related to the nature of the business and not all organisations will necessarily be able to achieve full operational level control over quality and productivity.

The extent to which Cashbuild managed to introduce such an integrated cyclic process of business has been a key factor in its transformation and success. Albert Koopman saw it like this: "Our business revolved around the contribution of every employee and to this end we had to spell out a few premises." These premises were, in brief:

1. Recognition that every employee was involved in the marketing process
2. Quality service was achieved through people
3. Higher productivity would be achieved by:
   * Changing the people who did the work
   * Redefining the way people worked
   * Giving job enrichment by changing the work people did.
4. Capturing the market could only be done by committed people.

Through the implementation of CARE groups and the VENTURECOMM system, Cashbuild was able to break down the barriers that segment departments and alienate people from one another. In so doing, they did not abdicate responsibility to workers but rather created a system of fairly transferring and sharing responsibility according to the expressed needs and abilities of the employees.

A further element of Cashbuild's success was that it did not pay lip-service to people participation. It actually instituted it as a way of life!

108

7) Giving the people a holistic, understandable organisational structure

As Drucker (1980) points out: "It is just as risky, just as arduous, and just as uncertain to do something small that is new as it is to do something big that is new."

Cashbuild took the risk of doing something big and created a completely new approach to organisational structure.

Figure 17 reproduces the Cashbuild pyramid (already illustrated in Part 1), so that we may discuss its features in some detail. Notice that the customer is at the apex with the employee, company and supplier/competitor at three of the base points. The focal point of the pyramid is the "extra mile", or employee commitment, whereby the other four components are integrated towards achieving corporate excellence.

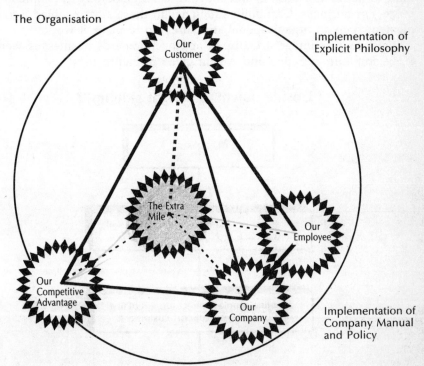

Figure 17: The Cashbuild organic structure

The similarity between this pyramidal organisational structure and the productivity barrel outlined in Figure 15 is apparent. The pyramidal structure moves away from the traditional hierarchy of cascading responsibility

p105

109

where the operational level has no real contact with, or responsibility towards the customer, supplier or success of the company as a whole.

In the pyramid concept, supplier and customer are regarded as integral parts of the organisation and the company can be viewed as the vehicle through which the people/employees are able to achieve a high level of excellence in quality and productivity. (This necessarily leads to profitability.)

For Cashbuild the "extra mile" is really what the business is all about. The extra mile is the commitment and involvement that every employee feels towards the core objectives and philosophies of the organisation. The extra mile is the factor that distinguishes mediocre from excellent performance and makes the difference between ultimate failure or success of an organisation.

It must be stressed that such an organisational structure is dependent on fluidity, debureaucratising, and above all participation by all people in the process of business. Cashbuild's initiative in these areas enabled it to implement such an organisational structure and to make it work.

Evidence of a similar structure or approach towards business is seen in the example from Peters and Austin given in Figure 18.

"Upside down" or "right side up"?

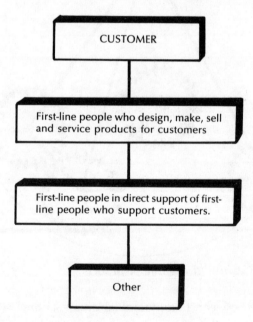

Figure 18: Reversing the organisational structure

110

The "upside down" chart is a simple depiction of business success. The customer comes first. First-line people in line functions who support him come next. Below them come first-line people in support functions and finally management.

Organisational structures are normally based on well-defined logical structures ensconced in multiple rules and regulations to help the manager and worker to cope with every conceivable situation. It is not surprising that in many organisations the customer becomes a secondary element as everybody jockies and battles to maintain his or her own little position in the ivory tower. As the research of Project Free Enterprise clearly indicated, very little attention is paid to the perceptions and participation of the people who are, in the final analysis, responsible for productivity in the business.

Cashbuild's obsession with people participation at all levels and its concern for the perceptions of its employees were probably the major motivating force behind the creation of its unique organisational structure. With all the criticism that could be levelled against this structure and approach, the important fact is that it worked for Cashbuild, and has worked for many other companies including the "excellent" companies quoted in the work of Peters, Austin and Waterman.

Meaning and human dignity

Many companies have embarked on the transformation route by spending vast amounts of money on improving hygiene factors such as the physical working environment, canteen facilities, etc. and on paying workers more acceptable salaries. In most of these cases the objective was to improve productivity while simultaneously wanting to improve the lot of the labour force. Many of these organisations were disappointed because there was no improvement in productivity - in fact they often recorded a decline in productivity and quality. Why did this occur? The answer is quite simply, that although these hygiene factors are important they are by no means the full answer.

Victor Frankl, one of the world's leading experts in human motivation, regards the primary driving force of man as being the search for meaning.

> Man is always reaching out for meaning, always setting out on his search for meaning: in other words, what I call the will to meaning is even to be regarded as man's primary concern.... It is precisely this will to meaning that remains unfulfilled by today's society - and disregarded by today's psychology. Current motivation theories see man as a being who is either reacting to stimuli or abreacting his impulses. If we are to bring out the human potential at its best we must first believe in its existence and presence. Otherwise man will drift, he will deteriorate for there is a human potential at worst as well (1959).

It would be an oversimplification of Frankl's work to assume that the workplace is the only venue where a man may find meaning in his life. But since most adults spend the greater part of their working lives in the job environment, finding meaning in one's job must have a profound effect on one's conception of the meaning of life.

In Cashbuild the following premise was adopted regarding its people: "The basic premise of Cashbuild's attitude towards its people is that they were born from human clay: each has his own rights, each is an individual, each has the will to work, each wants to have some control over his destiny."

Cashbuild based its transformation on the assumption that every employee is a human being with a right to assert his or her human dignity. Management was determined to create an environment in which the employee could feel himself to be part of a team which was working towards uplifting the knowledge, responsibility, involvement and standard of life of all its members - as well as towards fulfilling the company's goals.

Such people become the greatest allies of the business - they are the committed soldiers who fight the cause of war in a very efficient manner.

112

13

Formulating a strategy for organisational transformation and excellence

ie implementat⁻ of strategy.

For the last 25 or 30 years, the concept of planning has proved highly productive. One could assume a continuation of trends within fairly narrow ranges, rather than sudden sharp shifts. One could start out with today and project into the future ... one could assume that tomorrow would continue today, with a different mix perhaps but much the same basic configuration.

The most probable assumption today is the unique event, which changes the configuration drastically. Unique events cannot be planned. They can however be seen, or rather, one can prepare to take advantage of them. One can have strategies for tomorrow that anticipate the areas in which the greatest changes are likely to occur, strategies that enable a business to take advantage of the unforeseen and unforseeable (Drucker 1980).

can be but I difficult

Many organisations tend to regard strategy as an exercise of budgeting for the new year to come. In the companies that do think further ahead, most of them try to concentrate their strategy on financial and technical matters without taking into account the people who will in the end cause the strategy to succeed or fail.

trend

All businesses are human institutions, not plush buildings, bottom lines, strategic analysis, super technology or five year plans. Because people are energy sources, each with a unique personality, each holding a specific set of beliefs and values, each projecting a specific behaviour pattern, we can speak of a living organisation! Organisations with a long history of success, characterised by competent leadership and demonstrated excellence, appear

note

113

to have their real existence rooted in the hearts and minds of their employees (Baron 1986; Bennis & Nanus, 1985; Hickman & Silva, 1984; Deal & Kennedy, 1982; Peters & Waterman, 1982; Porter, 1975).

The planning of the hard variables such as operational expenses, future technology, budgeting, return on assets, is an essential part of strategy and is competently coped with by most organisations. Yet researchers (Sathe, 1985; Peters & Waterman, 1982; Deal & Kennedy, 1982) argue that there are four major variables that are critical to effective strategy formulation:

* Organisational structure and design
* The management process
* Human resources
* Organisational culture.

For an organisation to achieve its strategic objectives and accomplish its mission, all four variables require attention. The variable which seems to have received the least attention from the less successful organisations is organisational culture and its influence in shaping the internal organisational system towards excellence and improved productivity (Schmikl, 1985). For the sake of clarity culture can be defined as ''the way we do things around here'' (Bowers, 1966) or ''the process that ties people together and gives meaning and purpose to their day-to-day lives'' (Deal & Kennedy, 1982). The culture of an organisation therefore refers to the values, beliefs, ideals and symbols that have come to mean something to the people who work there.

Cashbuild, like many other businesses, did have a strategy but found that it was not working. Profits were falling and the business was no longer meeting its strategic objectives. At this stage Cashbuild embarked on research into what was hampering the growth of the business and came to the conclusion that it had to concentrate on developing a culture which was people sensitive.

In Albert Koopman's words: ''We saw however that in Cashbuild's case the formulation of our strategy revolved in the main around its people and the environment. Cashbuild thus opted for culture driving strategy and not strategy directing culture as is often the case in the typical South African company .... It was felt by Cashbuilders that to have committed soldiers (all employees) half trained in the use of the gun was superior to having fully skilled soldiers who were uncommitted to the cause (mission).''

This concentration on culture caused the Cashbuild management to place people and development of human potential above all else in creating the strategy of the future. From this key strategic objective flowed Cashbuild's unique organisational structure, design, participative management process,

114

and human resource policies. Profitability, good return-on-investments and a successful business were seen as by-products that would flow from having committed people who perceived themselves to have a real stake in the business.

Formulating strategy at Cashbuild

Cashbuild's executives asked themselves the question: "What do we need to do to enable us to ensure that we will still be around and successful in a post-apartheid society through to the year 2000?"

In attempting to answer that question, they involved over 200 people in discussing corporate strategy. Employees at all levels were asked to participate and state their views as perceived from their own organisational position. The belief was that no strategy could be formulated unless it *evolved* out of experience and included opinions from all incumbents. The one-page statement of belief that was finally distilled is reflected below:

Cashbuilders' "Statement of Belief"

* We offer superior value for money for our customers.
* We allow each employee to develop to his fullest human potential through good leadership.
* Our company strives to be the most cost efficient and well-run business in our industry.
* We continuously strive for cost effectiveness and competitive advantage through effective strategic thinking.
* We drive our business by going the "Extra Mile".

The strategic options which emerged were four-fold and gave management a springboard from which tactical plans could evolve :

* The customer
  Market penetration - how?
  * Increase customers
  * Increase quantity purchased
  * Increase frequency of purchase
  * Increase loyalty.

* The company
  Productivity improvement - how?
  * Increase price/margin
  * Improve merchandise mix
  * Alter fixed cost
  * Focus on cost curve
  * Variable cost adjustment.

CULTURE STRATEGY	OUR EMPLOYEE		
	AS WORKER/Commitment	AS INDIVIDUAL/Competency and Creativity	AS A TEAM/Cooperation
	Individual values and company goals are congruent and directed to common goals.	Company provides training and skills to improve the quality of worklife in the organisation.	Joint decision-making and participation at all levels to form an effective and cohesive team.
OUR CUSTOMER	*Commitment* at all times to giving the customer value for money. Commitment to the fact that he is "King".	Providing the customer with *competent* service to the benefit of all. With competency we build loyal customers and through training we build competency.	Through teamwork and effective participation we can *consistently* improve services rendered to the customer. Consistency builds repeat business.
OUR COMPETITOR	*Commitment* that we will at all times look for competitive advantages over our competitors and implementing these - **NOW!**	To formulate and apply new strategies against our competitor with *competency and creativity*. In this manner we can gain competitive advantage and give our business an edge.	As a team we must *consistently* look for new ways to beat the competition through our process of joint decision making. Never must we lose sight of the fact that competition might creep up on us one day.
OUR COMPANY	Every employee must show *commitment* to the Company. Its philosophies and policies must be congruent with individual values and goals so that we can build on our company strength with *commitment*.	Our company's strengths must be exploited and improved upon. If we execute our tasks with *competence* we will achieve this aim. Our company has to be the best.	We must, as a Team, *consistently* look for ways to capitalise on our company's strengths through a multitude of workshops and brainstorming sessions. Joint decisions on issues raised will improve the quality of our strategies in the longer term.

Figure 19: The interdependence of corporate culture and strategy of Cashbuild

* Competitor/competitive advantage
  Market development - how?
  • New geographic markets
  • New market segments
  • Focus on cost leadership.

* Employee
  Development of human potential - how?
  • Operational evolution
  • Customer/employee integration
  • Organisational development
  • The "cause" of our business
  • Mission
  • The way we develop committed people.

Because Cashbuild made the conscious choice that the corporate culture should determine strategy, rather than the other way around, they enjoyed an important strategic advantage in that "management focuses on the art rather than on the science of change management and leadership", as Koopman put it.

The philosophy reflected in Figure 19 is a living dogma for Cashbuilders. Again this was developed through participative consultation and has subsequently been translated into seven languages for all Cashbuilders to read. For anyone who is illiterate, the concepts are carefully explained by the manager and/or VENTURECOMM, so that he can fully understand and become a dedicated disciple of the Cashbuild mission.

Organisational cultures

The choice of a strategy, as has already been stated, is dictated by organisational culture. The strategies of worker participation cannot, therefore, be introduced into an organisation until it has brought about whatever cultural changes may be necessary to ensure that the strategies can actually be implemented.

There are many different definitions of organisational culture, but all focus upon the standard belief that values are the most important component of a corporate culture. These values are reflected in the way people do things and in the day-to-day living and management styles within the organisation. According to Schmikl corporate values tend to:

* Provide a sense of common direction for all employees, and serve as guidelines for day-to-day behaviour

* Show people how to work together - they can command their attention, influence their beliefs, and suggest standards they should live by.

Researchers Handy (1976), Schein (1983) and Sathe (1985) have identified four major kinds of organisational cultures:

* Power culture
* Personal culture
* Role/mechanistic culture
* Task/organic culture

For the purpose of this book we will be concentrating only on the role/mechanistic and task/organic cultures. The characteristics and differences of each are set out in Figures 20 and 21.

Cashbuild shifted from a role culture towards a task culture. Cashbuild's then operations manager, Gerald Haumant (now Koopman's successor as CEO) indicates the change in management style and culture in the following statement: ''Indeed the company has had a change in management style since its earlier days. The Managing Director used to be a very autocratic sort of person. He, however, saw the market changing, observed the aspirations of blacks and, because he is such a down-to-earth guy, picked up certain things he would have missed altogether if he were more of a status-minded corporate man. We moved from a very autocratic to a truly democratic company. Initially, in testing our concepts, strong discipline was inevitable. Once the formula was established these stringent controls were no longer necessary. Control is now self-motivated. More and more, instead of being involved in devising new control systems, management concentrates on the strategic issues of the business.''

The research that Cashbuild did to determine the feelings and perceptions of their workers enabled them to clearly identify the organisational climate and then to develop the type of culture that would facilitate the implementation of a participative strategy. This again reinforces the point that Cashbuild's strategy is driven by the culture of the system and its employees.

Lastly, cultures differ within functional organisation divisions, and there remains a need to become sensitive to the organisational culture so as to be able, through effective leadership, to foster and strengthen the corporate values that will induce employees at all levels to commit themselves to the organisation's goal. In this way strategy, culture, and management processes become effectively integrated. This kind of synergy leads to corporate excellence.

118

mechanistic   *organic*

The role culture

Is often stereotyped as bureaucratic.

This culture works by logic and rationality.

The role organisation rests its strengths on the pillars of its functional specialisations.

It is controlled by:

- Procedures for roles - job descriptions, authority definitions, key performance areas, etc.
- Procedures for communication roles for settlement of disputes, etc.

It is coordinated at the top by a narrow band of senior managers.

In this culture job descriptions are often more important than the individuals filling the job.

Individuals are selected for satisfactory performance of a role.

The role is so described that a number of people could fill or fit it. Performance over and above the role prescription is not required, and can be disruptive at times.

Positional power is the major source of power in this culture. Personal power is frowned upon and expert power tolerated in its correct place.

Rules and procedures are the major method of influence. Efficiency depends on the rationality of the allocation of work and responsibility rather than individual personality.

The role culture succeeds as long as this type of organisation operates in a stable environment.

The task culture

It is job or project oriented. Its structure is best represented as a net (networking).

Power is centred at the interstices and this culture is often found within matrix organisations.

The whole emphasis of the culture is on getting the job done. It seeks to bring resources together and style is important. Influence is based on expert power rather than positional or personal power although these cannot be ignored and do have their effect.

It is a team culture.

The task culture utilises the unifying power of the group to improve efficiency and to identify the individual with the organisation's objectives.

This culture is very adaptive and task forces can be formed for specific purposes, reformed, or abandoned.

Decision-making is contained in the group and individuals have a high degree of control over their work.

This culture is appropriate where flexibility and sensitivity to the market environment are important.

Found in competitive markets and where product life cycles are short.

Philosophy and vision are the sources of influence. Efficiency operates on recognising opportunities or responding to them by relying on self-discipline rather than external rules or procedures.

Task culture can succeed in unstable, dynamic environments.

Figure 20: Comparison of role/mechanistic and task/organic cultures

119

Role cultures offer the individual employee:	Task cultures offer the individual employee:
• Security and predictability. • Progress up the corporate ladder. • Opportunities to acquire specialist expertise. • Role cultures often depend on organisational structure rather than on individual capabilities.	• Determination of career advancement. • Security through innovation and team work. • Opportunities to acquire specialist expertise through personal involvement. • Reward for team effort.

Figure 21: Impact of role and task cultures on employees

Strategy and transformation

Every enterprise needs a mission - a specific purpose. Survival depends on it. However, that purpose must be realistic in terms of the desires of society, resources available, competition and technology. There must be a matching of hopes and practical objectives. Strategy is a tool that is devised to clarify such a mission and to harness human effort for the achievement of that mission. The development of a strategy and the achievement of organisational transformation are interdependent activities. It is unlikely that effective transformation will occur without a clearly defined mission and strategy. On the other hand the direction of the transformation will influence the strategy and will determine its success in its implementation.

There are, according to Warren and Newman (1982), four major qualities or characteristics usually present in successful strategy:

120

* The strategy guides the enterprise over a period of years. Time is need-ed to build up momentum.
* The strategy is quite selective in the points it emphasises. It focuses on key features which are important and regarded as providing a continu-ing basis of distinctiveness.
* The strategy is the dominant guide to action. It provides the overriding operating goals. Ideally the strategy permeates the entire organisation with a sense of mission.
* The strategy guides the relationship of the enterprise to both its external environment and its internal activities.

An organisation's strategy can be determined in a variety of ways. Mintz-berg states that an organisation can have a strategy even though no one ever systematically set one forth. For instance, strategy may grow out of a series of decisions regarding immediate problems: similarities in these de-cisions are gradually identified and accepted as norms which employees are expected to follow. If such emerging norms deal with strategic matters then the enterprise, in fact, does have a strategy which almost everyone follows. This type of informal, emerging strategy evolves in many organisations but there is the danger that a lack of clear direction and purpose could hamper the potential growth of the enterprise.

Another method of strategy formulation is through the intuitive decisions of a powerful individual. Usually, a strong leader does not explore many alternatives but is inclined to choose a direction through personal prefer-ence and intuition. Although many examples of this approach can be cited - Henry Ford and Howard Hughes - reliance on this intuitive method is very risky. The exit of the visionary leader or a loss of popularity and power on his behalf could plunge the organisation into chaos.

A strategy can also be determined through a systematic analysis of the current status of an organisation in relation to its mission and desired ob-jectives. This method is dependent on an effective process of consultation between all the disciplines and levels of responsibility within the organisa-tion in order to accurately determine the status quo. The direction of the strategy will therefore be determined by an analysis of the strengths and weaknesses, culture, availability of supplies, the strength of competition, the market, finances, etc.

Finally, the strategy of an organisation may be determined by a crisis or dilemma that may be confronting it. The nature of such a situation could motivate a business to embark on a process of transformation and new direction.

Cashbuild's transformation was precipitated by a crisis that was facing the organisation, and its current strategy was evolved through a mix of strong intuitive leadership and systematic analysis and consultation. Albert Koopman and his executive recognised and predicted a crisis for the organisation and embarked on a strategic direction that required a shift from traditional management to strong visionary leadership.

The success of the strategy and transformation was due to an ability to combine vision, intuition and leadership with a systematic analysis of the business, through a process of consultation with all the employees.

Transformation and the Strategic Development Curve

Effective strategy formulation and transformation depend on accurately analysing the current status of growth within an organisation. An incorrect assessment of either the macro or micro issues confronting an organisation can result in the right actions being taken at the wrong time, which will result in failure of the initiative.

The Strategic Development Curve provides a useful reference base from which to evaluate the status quo in an organisation. This reference forms the basis for assessing the nature and thrust of the required transformation process. Figure 22 clearly indicates the four basic phases of development with typical consequences which can be expected from any one position along this curve.

Although most executives and managements of organisations understand the need for growth and change, it is a fact that many fail to manage organisational development effectively. The discomfort of growth or the comfort of being in a specific phase translates into resistance to change and a focus on the past rather than on the future. It is this that causes companies to stagnate at a specific point in the process of development and to experience the disastrous effects of Phase 4 on the development curve.

Organisations often find it difficult to initiate new strategies on transformation at stages 1 and 3 on the development curve. This is due to the fact that initial efforts may, in fact, deliver negative returns. Figure 23 illustrates the relationship between investment of effort and the return that is achieved by the organisation. In this figure effort or investment is represented as the horizontal dimension while impact is reflected on the vertical dimension. Both are seen in relation to one another on the development curve.

It can be seen that the initial effort expended during Phase 1 will produce negative returns in the short term. This often causes organisations to abandon the initiative or to begin implementing *ad hoc* and incremental changes that they hope will give immediate short term, positive returns.

If an organisation manages to develop from Phase 1 to Phase 2 the return on effort starts to produce increasingly positive results. This is the phase characterised by a sense of buoyancy and optimum positive yields. This positive yield however decreases during Phase 3 of the development curve to

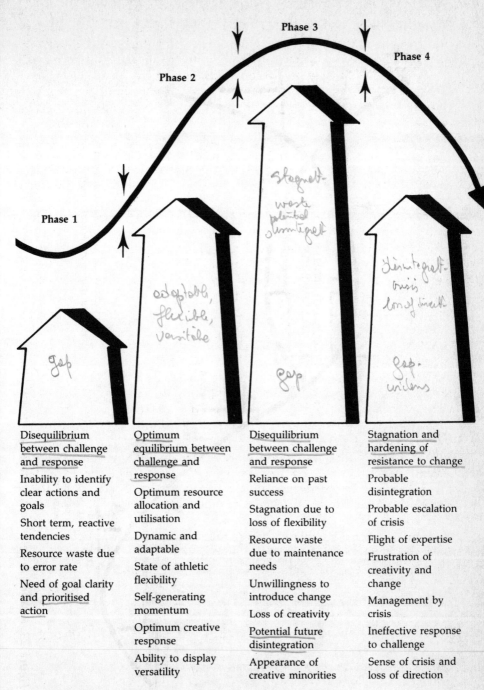

Phase 1	**Phase 2**	**Phase 3**	**Phase 4**
Disequilibrium between challenge and response	Optimum equilibrium between challenge and response	Disequilibrium between challenge and response	Stagnation and hardening of resistance to change
Inability to identify clear actions and goals	Optimum resource allocation and utilisation	Reliance on past success	Probable disintegration
Short term, reactive tendencies	Dynamic and adaptable	Stagnation due to loss of flexibility	Probable escalation of crisis
Resource waste due to error rate	State of athletic flexibility	Resource waste due to maintenance needs	Flight of expertise
Need of goal clarity and prioritised action	Self-generating momentum	Unwillingness to introduce change	Frustration of creativity and change
	Optimum creative response	Loss of creativity	Management by crisis
	Ability to display versatility	Potential future disintegration	Ineffective response to challenge
		Appearance of creative minorities	Sense of crisis and loss of direction

Figure 22: The Strategic Development Curve

123

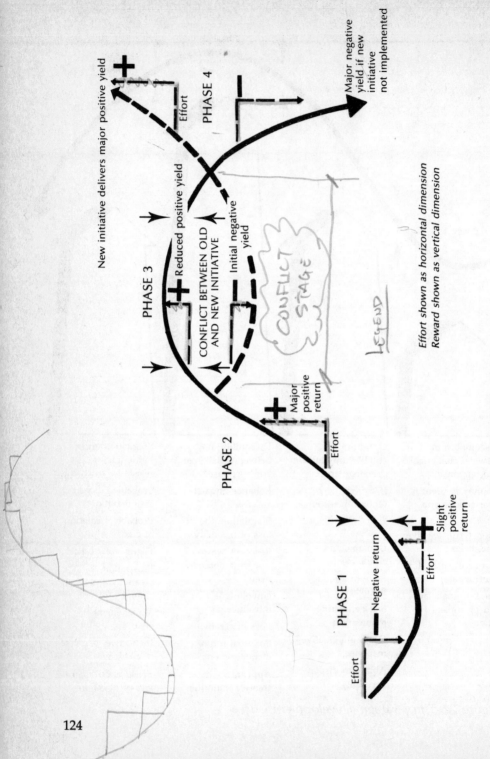

Figure 23: Reward in relation to phases of development

a point where effort is merely equal to the yield experienced. It is during Phase 3 that the organisation is confronted with the need to embark once again on new initiatives in order to address the disequilibrium between challenge and response.

The Phase 3 disequilibrium places the organisation in a situation where it must meet the dual requirements of:

* Maintaining and optimising aspects of Phase 2 that are still giving a positive return, while
* Embarking on new initiatives that may initially give a negative yield.

This phase will be characterised by conflict between the people who rely on past success and resist change, and the creative minority who focus on a vision and agitate for change and new directions.

A mechanistic, rigid organisational culture and structure that do not encourage entrepreneurship will tend to discourage the creative minorities and to suppress any new initiatives that would begin a new growth curve. This will cause the organisation to maintain systems and methods of operation that no longer effectively address the challenge and changing environment. It is at this stage that the organisation will go into Phase 4 of the development curve and start experiencing an increasingly negative return on output. The very same systems, actions and management style that produced such positive yields during Phase 2 now start to have a negative impact and the result is often one of confusion and chaos.

It must also be understood that once an organisation finds itself in Phase 4 it becomes increasingly more difficult to embark on any new strategic initiative or process of transformation. As the downward momentum increases, new efforts or attempts at transformation initially yield increasingly high negative returns. This results in symptoms of stagnation, flight of expertise, management by crisis, ineffective response to challenge and eventual disintegration of the system.

Figure 24 illustrates Cashbuild's current status of growth and its development over the past five years. Historical development status and major actions are well reflected on this growth curve.

Tracing Cashbuild's development as shown in Figure 24

1978
Origin of the business.

1979
Small profits were made.

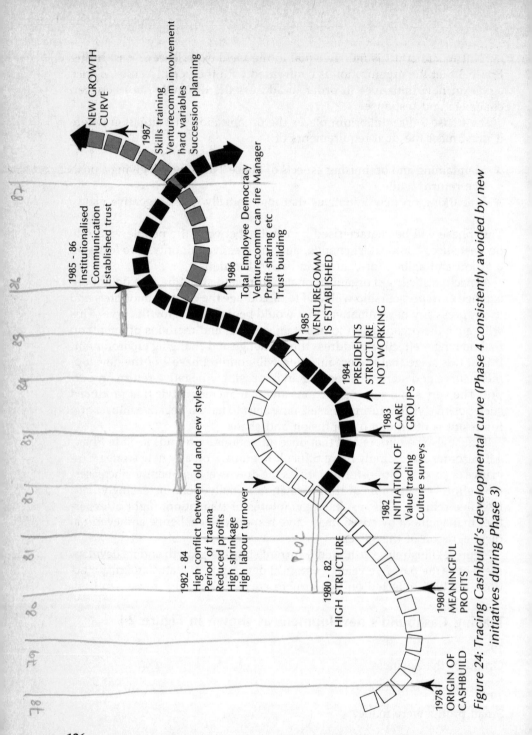

Figure 24: Tracing Cashbuild's developmental curve (Phase 4 consistently avoided by new initiatives during Phase 3)

NEW GROWTH CURVE

1987
Skills training
Venturecomm involvement
hard variables
Succession planning

1985 - 86
Institutionalised
Communication
Established trust

1986
Total Employee Democracy
Venturecomm can fire Manager
Profit sharing etc
Trust building

1985
VENTURECOMM
IS ESTABLISHED

1984
PRESIDENTS
STRUCTURE
NOT WORKING

1983
INITIATION OF
CARE
GROUPS

1982
INITIATION OF
Value trading
Culture surveys

1982 - 84
High conflict between old and new styles
Period of trauma
Reduced profits
High shrinkage
High labour turnover

PLOC

1980 - 82
HIGH STRUCTURE

1980
MEANINGFUL
PROFITS

1978
ORIGIN OF
CASHBUILD

1980

Generation of meaningful profits.

1980 - 1982

* The organisation was structured according to traditional structures where people were "boxed" into specific functions and not given room to be innovative or to really participate in the running of the business.
* This period was also characterised by an autocratic style of management by Koopman and his team.
* The business was run in a traditional PLOC style, i.e. rational management processes that alienated the workers from management and the objectives of the business.

1982

The following symptoms of Cashbuild's tumble became visible:

* Reduction of profits
* High shrinkage (1,4%)
* High labour turnover (126%)
* Conflict between management and workers
* Negative worker perception about the business.

Koopman identified the need to change the management style and culture of the business to address this problem.

1982 - 1984

This period was characterised by value trading, a shift in culture, and preparation of the new business environment. A system for participation was designed. Vast energy was expended toward establishing worker participation through the CARE groups and Presidents' structure. This initiative, however, still gave negative returns for the first two years because sufficient trust had not developed between workers and management, and the presidents were rejected by the workers. The need for a wider involvement became apparent and a vote of confidence was sought from a larger front of workers. Workers were asked to participate in designing the VENTURECOMM system.

1985

* VENTURECOMM (as designed by the workers) was implemented as a result of a vote of confidence by employees (95% in favour) as the "way of life" or system of participation they wanted.

* Portfolio members were democratically elected and their tasks designed by themselves (concentrating on the strategic "soft variables" of the business).
* A "creed of trust" was developed jointly by management and employees.
* An internal marketing drive by management was launched to reinforce the "new way of life" of Cashbuild.
* At this stage a negative response was experienced from "white management" in reaction to the empowerment of employees. A certain degree of malicious compliance (covert resistance) was experienced from less mature managers.
* The translated philosophy was compiled in booklet form and distributed to all employees.

1986

* Through joint decision-making, VENTURECOMM workers were drawn into the processes of the business, concentrating on the implementation of soft variable decisions.
* Launching of a massive interactional skills training programme for all levels.
* Design by workers of all the concomitant reward systems.
* Total empowerment of workers to remove individuals (including management) who transgressed the principles of the Cashbuild philosophy. Management's discretionary "rule of law" was effectively removed. The process was however always the outcome of full employee democracy.
* This empowerment of workers forced managment to adopt a more leadership oriented role. Effectively, a vote of confidence was made by management in workers and by workers in management. Trust barriers had effectively been removed.

1987

* Participation in soft variable processes became a way of life and the Phase 3 optimisation of worker trust and involvement was achieved.
* A new initiative (i.e. new Phase 1 of growth) was launched to focus on the transfer of hard variable skills to the workforce. Rather than working on trust building and individual needs, workers now addressed the functional productivity and quality problems of the business.

Cashbuild experienced negative returns on considerable effort and expenditure in the initial launching of the new strategy in 1982. In the words of the personnel manager, George Bell: "When we started out it was pay, pay, pay. Everything centred around the needs of the workers and they spoke

128

consistently about problems with uniforms, overtime, loans, safety items, etc. Initially, very little was said about productivity and how to reduce shrinkage and all the other items that management would have liked them to talk about.''

Cashbuild paid for research to determine the perceptions of its workforce. Workshops were conducted continually throughout the country, at the cost of hundreds of valuable man-hours, to determine the philosophy and strategy of the organisation; management carried the expense of improving hygiene factors and of working towards resolving the legitimate grievances of employees; money was spent on the training and development of people to enable them to contribute meaningfully in the future. All this without any initial improvement in productivity or real positive short term return on investment.

Yet management stuck to the philosophy and vision which enabled Cashbuild to develop the kind of entrepreneurial drive and organic flexibility that would produce the positive yields reflected in Phase 2 of the development process, and to implement new measures which would address future challenges during Phase 3.

14

Participative management: From CARE to VENTURECOMM

Excellent organisations have, according to Peters and Austin (1985), been distinguished by their ability to listen and trust and respect the dignity and creative potential of each person in the organisation. This implies that participation is a key to organisational success.

In 1986 more than 120 of South Africa's leading organisations participated in "Project Free Enterprise". Its basic objective was to determine how every South African could participate in and be committed to the concept of a growing economy in this country. Some 2 000 workers, managers and executives took part in identifying the macro and micro priorities for generating the solutions to enhance economic participation in South Africa. By far the most important item to emerge was the issue of participation in the workplace. Time and again, this has been identified as central to creating cohesion between management and workforce, and to achieving levels of commitment that would otherwise not be possible. Management agrees that participation is furthermore essential in developing a quality orientation. This, together with commitment to the mission of the organisation, would make for unparalleled corporate performance. The findings of "Project Free Enterprise" indicate that the participative systems being used are still, by and large, in an exploratory and immature stage of development. In many companies there is a marked discrepancy between the perceptions of workers and management regarding how much actual worker involvement is, in fact, being allowed.

Management also tends to be satisfied with broad generic statements of intent rather than the implementation of specific action plans. This is compounded by the fact that managers often pay lip-service to issues such as black advancement and incentives for excellence while allowing very little actual innovation or advancement for their black employees. It was further evident from the study that top and senior management's intentions are not properly communicated down the line and are therefore less than credible at the lower levels. The commitment to participative systems and management is also often a boardroom decision which is invariably not practised by first line supervisors.

We have already enumerated the core principles of implementing and maintaining a participative system. A number of these are more fully developed in this section, but before proceeding with this, we reiterate that unless *all* these core principles are incorporated into the strategy and ultimately into the system, no innovation will work.

Participation is a process

Cashbuild's success has been characterised by an on-going process of development and striving towards excellence. As in other companies which have distinguished themselves as excellent organisations, Cashbuild's management realised that excellence could only be achieved through the commitment and involvement of all the people in the business. This type of commitment, dedication, involvement and excellence can only be achieved when management understands and accepts that participation is a process and not a single act or event.

Western managers, in general, seem to concern themselves with solving problems and manipulating events in order to achieve given budgets within a particular financial calendar. Their focus is on what acts they need to perform in order to force unexpected and unwanted events or symptoms back into predictable and controllable sequences. A system of worker participation cannot be brought about in this way. The Cashbuild story of innovation, evaluation by means of workshops and seminars and indabas, followed by further innovation and modification, followed yet again by feedback and evaluation, makes it abundantly clear that Koopman and his team accepted participation as a process, an ongoing way of life.

Top management commitment

As with any other aspect of the business plan, the success of the participative system in an organisation is heavily dependent on the level and intensity of top management commitment. As Toyota's Colin Adcock puts it: "If it (participation) were a religion, management would have to be its disciples." Elsewhere it has been stated that participative management needs champions to drive it and see it as a total way of life. Regardless of the size or nature of the business, senior management and its cohorts have to be perceived to be champions of the cause if it is to become a way of life within the organisation.

It is true to say that in most organisations human resource strategies, and consequently participative systems, do not form part of the total business plan. These aspects are left to human resources specialists who often lack the necessary power or credibility with line functions to ensure their effective implementation. The formulation of integrated strategies around issues such as human resource development and involvement is still fairly uncommon in the South African environment.

Excellent companies are inclined to focus their efforts and strategies around the key element of human resources. In the not-so-excellent, financial systems, technological advancement, product development, administrative and control systems, investment etc., are aspects of the strategy that are well advanced, while employee involvement in productivity and quality remain in an embryonic stage of development.

In excellent companies which have developed effective participative systems, top management has been involved in setting the basic framework and overall objectives of participation as part of the integrated business plan. The finer issues around the implementation requirements, difficulties, time frames and responsibilities are however elicited from line management. This follows the creed of: "The man who implements the plan must design the plan". The involvement of line management at the earliest stages of strategy formulation is seen as a key priority for ensuring ultimate success.

Top management commitment to participative systems must go further than a declaration of intent to include another paragraph in the mission statement. It must be visible through actions and deeds, through visible signs of active management such as MBWA - active management by walking around. From the chief executive down managers need to walk around interacting with their staff and visibly living and marketing the message of participation. At Cashbuild, Albert Koopman, personnel manager George Bell, regional managers and the like, made a point of engaging in personal discussion with workers at the operational level. Here they listened to ideas, suggestions or complaints and negotiated joint solutions for the issues of the day.

The dedication of the senior executive and top management to developing the trust which allows for participation can be seen in their willingness actually to be champions of the cause. Peters and Austin (1985) quote Zaphiropaulos of Xerox as saying:

> There is basically one killer of successful and productive symbiosis, and that is contempt. Contempt tarnishes one's self image. It is also a deadly blow to a person's ego. Criticism should not include contempt. The

most commonly practised crime in industry today is a fundamental insensitivity toward personal dignity. False fronts are one way of displaying contempt. Private parking places are contemptuous towards those who do not have them.

Peters and Austin (1985) also cite the words of a senior executive of the automotive industry who said:

> I've never seen people in a factory angry because they were making $19 000 while the plant manager was making $70 000. What makes them furious, what demotivates and demoralises, is that slushy January 26 morning when they arrive for their shift at 4.45 am. They park their cars 100 yards away amidst the mud, dirt and slush and then they wander in, finally entering cold and wet through the door that's right next to the plant manager's empty parking spot. That's what certifies them as non full-scale adult human beings.

Koopman took the step of removing the signs which reserved specific parking spots for the chairman and directors. He replaced these with signs which read: "First come, first served". The result was that suddenly people started arriving at work earlier to claim the best parking spots - and timekeeping improved! Koopman also went further; he exchanged his high-status company car for one which allowed the workforce to identify with him more readily. These actions enabled him to earn the respect and trust of his workforce which in turn created in them a loyalty and commitment toward achieving excellence in the company.

Developing a philosophy

Fundamental to the success of Cashbuild has been the development of a philosophy which reflects and institutionalises the focus on people and their involvement at the core of the business. It is based on the development of human potential and the recognition of human dignity above all else. As indicated in earlier chapters, this philosophy has created for Cashbuild a vision that removes barriers between management, workers, the company, the customers and suppliers alike.

Core philosophies are a feature common to organisations that have distinguished themselves as "excellent". Jimmy Tribeck of Tandum Computers, for example, espouses the following philosophy:

1. All people are good.
2. People, workers, management and company are all the same thing.
3. Every single person in the company must understand the essence of the business.

133

4. Every employee must benefit from the company's success.
5. You must create an environment where all the above can happen.

The staff of Jet Stores (1986) in Durban have developed the following creed, which they call their "Family Ties" and which is what they live and work by:

1. Honesty is the best policy.
2. All people are good.
3. Customers are our salary.
4. United we stand.
5. Work smarter not harder.
6. Treat others as you wish to be treated.
7. Think first - then communicate.
8. Forgive and forget.
9. Be loyal to the Company.
10. Keep on smiling.

A strong people-oriented philosophy was a core element in the transformation of the Teleflex Engineering Company:

1. People are people, not personnel.
2. People don't dislike work, help them to understand mutual objectives and they'll drive themselves to unbelievable excellence.
3. The best way to really train people is with an experienced mentor on the job.
4. People have ego and development needs and they will commit themselves only to the extent that they can see ways of satisfying these needs.
5. People cannot be truly motivated by anyone else ... that door is locked on the inside; they should work in an atmosphere that fosters self-motivation, self-assessment and self-confidence.
6. People should work in a climate that is challenging, invigorating and fun ... and the rewards should be related as directly as possible to performance.
7. When people are in an atmosphere of trust, they'll put themselves at risk: only through risk is there growth, reward, self-confidence and leadership.

This type of philosophy assumes that the most important element of success in any business is the commitment of its people. In many excellent com-

134

panies winning strategies have flowed from similar philosophies. It is important to realise that a philosophy based on people and human dignity is not developed and adhered to for purely altruistic reasons. It makes good economic sense to live by a people-driven philosophy because it is only people who can then drive a business to excellence. Similarly people encase an organisation in mediocrity when they feel their spirit and dignity are being demeaned within the organisation.

Prepare the environment

No philosophy, strategy, action or decision, however good and well meant, can survive in an environment that is hostile.

Creating an environment that will be conducive to participative systems and management is as important as the structure of the system itself. Many organisations have had the painful and expensive experience of developing a theoretically perfect structure or model for participative systems which has failed dismally when implemented. Such failure has often been the outcome of management's lack of understanding of the perceptions and aspirations of the workforce. The workforce needs to believe that the system is intended to involve employees in the workings of the organisation and that it will provide a better and more meaningful quality of worklife for everyone. If it is seen as an extension of management's exploitation of the worker, the whole system is doomed to failure.

The argument from management is invariably that they are fully convinced of the importance of human dignity and employees' participation, and that if the workforce perceives this to be otherwise this is, indeed, unfortunate. The reality, however, is that it is the perceptions of the workforce that actually drive behaviour - often in a negative direction.

It is often the case that two groups (such as management and the workforce) hold totally different perceptions about the same issue. In such circumstances it is less important to argue about whose perception is right or wrong, than to concentrate on creating a mutual understanding of each other's perceptions. The focus then shifts to creating a common purpose based on common perceptions, which will drive both parties towards a common objective. This occurs through the simple process of value trading.

The stability and growth of any relationship are furthered when both parties work towards an understanding of each other's perceptions. This understanding forms the basis for ongoing negotiation and communication about establishing common goals regarding the future. This does not mean that people must become the same, or relinquish or suppress their own identity and unique vision of the world. It suggests rather that through an understanding of the other party's point of departure, it becomes possible to discover common interests and to acquire new behaviour patterns which

135

enable both parties to live together in harmony. Understanding each other's perceptions in the workplace enables both worker and manager to harness their energies towards the attainment of positive goals. The successful introduction of participative systems will depend on the extent to which management and workers understand each other's perceptions of life both within and outside the organisation. Managers who respect the dignity of the workpeople and perceive them to be making a valuable contribution towards the business must demonstrate this overtly. In other words, managers will have to actively involve workers in decisions, allow them to experiment and innovate, allow errors in decisions as part of the growth process and show interest in workers' needs and ideas by walking around and maintaining meaningful contact. Given this type of environment and understanding the worker is likely to grow more interested in participation, and his enthusiasm will begin to change his perception of exploitation by management. Common perceptions regarding the importance of self-worth and respect for the other's human dignity now become a common purpose which channels the energy of both parties towards mutual growth and success.

The Cashbuild management encountered hostility in the early stages of the transformation process. Koopman and his executives handled this, in part, by going to great lengths to demonstrate their own good faith. They saw to it themselves that requests and demands put forward by the CARE groups were effectively and promptly dealt with. No complaint was too petty to be listened and attended to. Problem situations were tackled on a person-to-person basis, no matter how inconvenient this may have been. In addition, the hostility was considerably dissipated by means of workshops at which people gradually felt free to express their feelings of resentment.

Guidelines for assessing the internal environmental climate

In order to avoid the pitfall of misjudging workers' attitudes towards the organisation, and attempting to introduce a participative system into a hostile environment, management must inform itself about the overall feeling in the workplace and about the individual issues which produce and perpetuate this feeling. This can only be done by ascertaining how workers perceive the organisation. The importance of this has already been stressed, and at this point we shall simply set out an outline of the steps that should be taken in conducting an effective survey of worker perceptions.

Step 1: Top management commitment to action

A feature which makes a survey of worker perceptions particularly attractive is that it is the most mechanistic facet of the integrated micro strategy.

It is therefore possible to implement a study of worker perceptions very rapidly without running the risk of making too many errors during the implementation stage. However, establishing what workers' perceptions are without a concomitant implementation of problem-solving actions could have more negative than positive effects. It is for this reason that Schmikl ( ) emphasises that top management must be totally committed to *utilising* the results of such surveys. Management must, therefore, understand that worker perceptions are not a figment of the imagination but are a reality for the individual worker. Once worker perceptions have been established, management must then accept them as a reality, as one version of the truth.

Step 2: Define project scope
Management must determine the scope of the research prior to starting the attitude survey. This means answering questions such as: do we need to determine perceptions in-house only, externally, or should we work on a combination of both internal and external perceptions? Do we wish to measure attitudes towards management, towards industrial relations, towards dissatisfiers and satisfiers within the organisation, towards the organisation in general, or towards departments in particular, or perhaps to determine perceptions for a combination of the above? This is vital, since many of the off-the-shelf attitude surveys are so structured that they may miss the very essence on which management chooses to focus.

Step 3: Orientate line management
Often noted is the potential resistance at the line management interface which can readily sabotage even the most well-intentioned initiative. For this reason emphasis has to be placed on preparation of the corporate environment, by discussing with line managers the motivation behind determining worker perceptions. This is of particular importance because line managers could very easily feel threatened by the potential ''exposure'' of such surveys. Once again, the success of resolving the problems highlighted by the survey will depend upon line managers' willingness to accept and monitor perceptions on an on-going basis.

Step 4: Questionnaire design
The use of foreign attitude measuring instruments in the South African context is often invalid - particularly at the lower levels in the organisation. Research conducted by Nasser, Nel, Schmikl and others has clearly indicated that much of the terminology which may be in common usage in the United States and Britain is foreign to South Africans. It is particularly important to take cognizance of language and sentence structure when measuring attitudes and perceptions of a group of people whose literacy levels

137

may cover a very wide range.

A further problem is encountered in determining the intensity of a perception. The generally accepted method relies upon asking respondents to evaluate situations on a scale, usually a five or seven point scale. South African research has again shown that unskilled and semiskilled respondents tend not to differentiate between finer shades of opinion and respond better to extreme positions, e.g. something is viewed as being either good or bad. For this reason it is necessary to develop and validate questionnaires around a three point scale, e.g. acceptability, non-acceptability and neutrality. Further dimensions may be included for "don't know" or "not applicable".

A great deal of care has to be taken to ensure that the questionnaire is validated in terms of what it is supposed to be measuring. The content of a question may in fact not be indicative of the attitude or perception which it is supposedly measuring. Surveys which are "loaded" to highlight preselected areas of concern often do little more than destroy the credibility of the process since these formats give invalid or biased information which is often misleading.

Step 5: Managing the literacy problem
A large proportion of the unskilled and semiskilled labour force is at best semiliterate. Questionnaires are of little use here. The only way of resolving the problem is to use trained interviewers on a face-to-face basis. Unfortunately, this involves the loss of the anonymity that is crucial to eliciting honest responses. It adds a further problem in that the interviewer's own perceptions, opinions and biases may influence the results. This makes it necessary to train carefully selected interviewers to a high degree of expertise. It is usually more acceptable to use external interviewers to determine worker perceptions.

Step 6: Utilisation of random samples
In most instances it is neither economical nor necessary to include all employees in a survey. South African research has indicated that the application of random and stratified samples gives accurate and valid results. Care needs to be taken to ensure that the sample is representative. Some organisations prefer to include every substantial individual in organisational surveys, as this prevents the possibility of rejection or suspicion of the results among those not included in the survey.

Step 7: Plan for post-survey action
The best results have been achieved in organisations where basic structures for implementing whatever action becomes necessary as a result of the

research, have been put into place prior to conducting the research. Sufficient time, responsibility and accountability allocations and monitoring procedures are necessary to ensure that actions are carried out with an optimum chance of success. Such a state of readiness prevents unnecessary delays or the rationalisation of survey results.

Step 8: Conduct survey and implement action
The time span between determining worker perceptions and the implementation of action is a key variable. The longer the delay between the survey itself and the visible implementation of action, the greater the chance of failure. Timely action creates trust, and develops a perception that management does in fact take the opinions of its workers seriously.

Going all the way

During September and October of 1986 a series of workshops was conducted throughout South Africa in a follow-up initiative to Project Free Enterprise. Representatives from over 120 organisations participated. Project Economic Participation, as it was called, defined an integrated strategy of five interrelated facets evolved from the workshops. One of these facets related to the concept of organisational solidarity. According to Nel (1987): "Solidarity or solidarism as it has now become known in the USA and Central America, defines a system of total productivity and quality development. It focuses on the democratization of capital and the fulfilment of the aspirations and needs of businessmen and workers alike. The objectives are:

1. to convert the company into a visible example of co-existing with others and to further the integral development of the workers;
2. to strengthen solidarity and goodwill relations between employers and employees;
3. to promote the workers' economic progress by improving the standards of living of their families and communities;
4. to foster social awareness in order to achieve greater justice and better understanding;
5. to promote the development of programmes orientated towards strengthening the integral development of the workers and their families;
6. to promote the company's productivity and yield for the benefit of everyone by involving employees in the decision-making process of the business;
7. above all, turn each individual into a stakeholder in the business."

139

Participants in Project Economic Participation further suggested the following operational guidelines:

* Implement organisational processes and philosophies which will nurture interdependent rather than independent or confrontational relationships with organised labour
* Involve labour (organised or otherwise) in all decisions which may affect their work or lives
* Develop participative management techniques and small group activities
* Introduce reward systems that offer employees a direct stake in organisational performance
* Implement processes that place people and the development of human potential above all else
* Develop organisational transparency which makes all employees a party to company performance goals, development etc.

Project Economic Participation went on to identify the following as key elements in an integrated strategy geared to help business meet the challenges of the future:

* Equal Opportunity Programmes (creating a business environment within which people of all races have effective access to opportunities inside the business)
* Political sensitisation (a systematic and orchestrated effort to initiate personal contact and dialogue between black and white, and management, in order to foster respect for basic human rights and dignity regardless of race, colour, sex or creed)

It can be seen from this that many other organisations in South Africa are aware of the need to develop processes within their businesses which will ensure communal ownership over the means of production and the evolution of democratic structures of self-control. Although many of them have set out on the road to implementing these principles most are still reluctant to move towards a true participative democracy in the workplace. In most cases businesses are still inclined to apply *ad hoc* actions that focus on effects of the problem rather than adopting holistic strategies that will address the causes.

Perhaps Cashbuild's greatest asset has been its willingness to go all the way toward implementing what South African management has been talking about for so long without actively moving towards implementation.

15
Adaptation and leadership

The growing alienation between management and the workforce has been the point of discussion in our previous chapters. The development of a highly structured impersonal culture, riddled with controls, has created an environment in which alienation has become the order of the day. In the typical organisation, management claims that it has a right to control within the system. This right to control translates into an imperious and autocratic management style in which management reserves the right over power, decision-making, authority, accountability, innovation and the dissemination of information. Caught up in the complexities of a large organisation, management feels justified in creating complex systems of control over the means of production. Rigid control systems are in turn administered by layer upon layer of managers each with their own well-defined and legitimised roles and authorities.

The assumption that management has the exclusive right to control, reduces the operational level or workforce to subservient implementors of management objectives and edicts. Robbed of any control over their own destinies, workers unite to regain their feeling of personal dignity and a share in the right to control the means of production.

This traditional alienation between management and workforce is characterised by management complaining of declining worker productivity, poor morale, lack of quality workmanship, absenteeism, labour turnover and a loss of loyalty toward the organisation and its objectives. The employees' response is that they have little or no real say regarding their work, motivation is lacking, their intelligence and experience are overlooked and underutilised and they are treated like machines in a work process which has little respect for their human dignity and personal aspirations. Although many organisations accurately identify the consequences of this alienation between management and the workforce, they are unable or unwilling to make the necessary adjustments to their structures and culture which will enable them to resolve the problem.

Changing the culture and structure of an organisation requires a decision of major proportions which will require a high degree of dedication and effort from all parties involved. Simple maintenance management is thus usually preferred to the perceived complexities of the participative system. Management is quick to point out that the corporate success over the past twenty years has been due largely to structures (autocratic) and centralised management - so why should it change now?

The reality, of course, is that success from the past is no predictor of success in the future. The challenges have changed and organisations are discovering that the old way of doing things often no longer works. Participation is by no means the only part of the formula in resolving the many challenges that face business. Poor productivity, low quality and lack of commitment from the workforce demand a multifaceted management approach in order to resolve this complex set of problems. It is significant to note, however, that many of the excellent companies who obtain above average performance, attribute their success to the high levels of involvement and commitment from their employees.

Meeting the challenge of future growth and prosperity will, for many organisations, mean the discomfort of shifting from traditionally centralised management structures towards more fluid, organic and participative modes of leadership.

In his article on "Revolt against working smarter", Soporito (1986) states that the consensus among academics, consultants and managers is that most efforts to introduce participation never make it. Cooke, a major authority on the subject, concludes that about 75% of all participative programmes in the 1980s failed in the United States. The reason for this failure can be directly attributed to management at all levels within the organisation.

> The concept was banished at the shop floor and even if it flourished there, was never permitted to creep higher. Jump on the quality circle bandwagon? Sure - takers were everywhere. But change the behaviour of managers or the organisational structure? Not this decade, thanks. The price of failure to establish a boilerroom to boardroom network of committed participative managers: shattered circles, confusion among the survivors and the same old mis-communication between the ranks.

Peters and Austin also indicate that the failure of businesses to enhance productivity and achieve high levels of quality and commitment from their workforce is the fault of management rather than the workers.

142

People all over the world think that it is the factory worker that causes the problems. He is not your problem. Ever since there has been anything such as industry, the factory worker has known that quality is what will protect his job. He knows that poor quality in the hands of the customer will lose the market and cost him his job. He knows it and lives with that fear every day - yet he cannot do a good job. He is not allowed to do it because the management wants figures, more products and often at the expense of quality. They measure only in figures. The factory worker is forced to make defective products, forced to turn out defective items. He is forced to work with defective material, so no matter what they do it will still be wrong. The worker cannot do anything about it. He is totally helpless. If he tries to do something about it, he might as well talk to the wall. Nobody listens.

The failure or refusal by many organisations to make the necessary cultural conversion is centred around the old issue of authority. Although workers leap at the opportunity to become more involved, management refuses to let go of its right to control.

Cashbuild experienced this very problem with managers who were initially reluctant to allow the workforce to participate fully in the process of the business. On the other hand employees displayed a much higher level of enthusiasm and commitment about bridging the gap and reducing the alienation between themselves, management and the company. Koopman had started off with an autocratic management style. But he saw the market changing, observed the aspirations of blacks and, because of an inherent perceptiveness, he picked up certain things that would otherwise have been missed entirely. Together with his senior management team, he moved from the autocratic mode towards a truly democratic stance. As Gerald Haumant (Koopman's successor as CEO of Cashbuild) puts it: ''We still have controls but they happen with minimum input from our side. They are self-enforced now, whereas they used to be pushed onto people. Through training and making people responsible and giving them a say, this was changed. They feel so much more part of it now. More and more instead of being involved in devising new control systems, management is leaving the tactical aspects of the business to the workforce and expending its valuable energy on the strategic issues that confront Cashbuild.''

From management to leadership

Once democracy in the workplace has been achieved, one enters the domain of freedom of association, freedom of speech and a host of other critical values. These values are different to those of dependence, submission and resignation which are more inclined to characterise the coercive or autocratic type of business. They reflect leadership.

143

Leadership is born from "walking among the people" assessing mood shifts, organisational climate, observing behaviours and reading attitudes. The leader's ability to interpret the creativity of the people he serves is crucial. This creativity is used to implement key strategies and help them through the value system change process. This is a new and different role from the the traditional controlling role of management. In his *Re-inventing the Corporation* Naisbitt says:

> The new corporation differs from the old in both goals and basic assumptions. In the industrial era, when the strategic resource was capital, the goal of the corporation could only have been profit.
>
> In the information era, however, the strategic resource is information, knowledge, creativity. There is only one way a corporation can gain access to these valuable commodities - i.e. through the people in whom these resources reside.
>
> So the basic assumption of a re-invented company is that people/human capital are its most important resource. What used to be the radicals' favourits slogan, 'people before profits,' is finding its way into the boardroom and being transformed into a more businesslike but equally humanistic 'people and profits'.

Naisbitt (1985), like Peters and Austin (1985), Drucker (1985), Schein (1970), Bennis (1985), Zaleznik (1977) and many other eminent researchers on excellence agree that the shift of focus in successful companies is towards more effective leadership of people rather than good management of capital and resources. As in many other excellent companies, Cashbuild has found that well-led people produce excellence in all other strategic areas of the business. Zaleznik, of Harvard University, asks the question:

> Is there a basic truth lurking behind the need for leaders that no matter how competent managers are, their leadership stagnates because of their limitations in visualising purposes and generating value in work? Without this imaginative capacity and the ability to communicate, managers, driven by their narrow purposes, perpetuate group conflicts instead of reforming them into broader desires and goals.

We have made the statement that Cashbuild's success was greatly due to the ability of Koopman and his executive team to become leaders rather than managers in the traditional sense of the word. This shift from management to leadership introduced a movement towards an innovative adaptable and organic culture that allowed and, in fact, encouraged all the people in the business to contributed toward its success. Again, it is Zaleznik who asks the fundamental question:

144

What about leaders, what do they do? Where managers act on limited choices, leaders work in the opposite direction, to develop fresh approaches to long standing problems and to open issues for new options. Stanley and Ingir Hoffman, political scientists, likened a leader's work to that of an artist. But unlike most artists, the leader himself is an integral part of the end product. One cannot look at the art without looking at the artist - in this case the leader. He is after all an integral part of the process.

Zaleznik identifies a further element that distinguishes managers from leaders, and that is their relationship with other people.

> Managers relate to people according to the role they play in a sequence of events or in a decision-making process, while leaders, who are concerned with ideas, relate in more initiating and empathetic ways. The manager's orientation to people, as actors in a sequence of events, deflects his or her attention away from the substance of people's concerns and towards their roles in a process. The distinction is simply between a manager's attention on how things get done and a leader's to what the events and decisions mean to participants.

Quite simply the manager focuses on doing things right. The leader is concerned with doing the right things. The difference is, running a business by a host of manuals and rules drawn up in the boardroom, as opposed to a simple visionary philosophy that is based on human dignity and lives in the hearts of the people.

A summary of the leadership qualities that facilitate participation
A leader must have the ability to interpret and to harness the creativity of the people he serves in order to implement a few key strategies to develop followership, as well as helping them through the value system change process. These qualities are translated to action by the following.

Displaying leadership
In essence a leader must:

* Change from autocratic rule and the non-understanding of human needs to developing flexibility and versatility in order to facilitate the change process
* Let go of viewing people as extensions to machines and become sensitive to the employee and his environment
* Forego his obsession with putting out fires for shareholders and start focusing on pleasing employees and customers

145

* Develop an internal locus of control in order to become proactive rather than an external locus of control and being reactive
* Become visionary by discarding static measurable absolutes and coming to grips with dynamic quantum leaps and paradigm shifts.

Empowering the worker and self-deployment of people development

Unless a leader knows himself first, he will never come to know his fellow man or develop personal power. He must "deploy" himself through other people through a change process. To facilitate this he needs to:

* Develop a sense of worth in his people
* Allow the worker to exercise the right of expectation, aspiration and fulfilment
* Constitutionalise justice in the organisation system
* Shift the emphasis to self-discipline rather than control

All the above enhance dignity in order to give expression to initiative and creativity while pursuing the work ethic.

Establishing cause, aspiration and vision

A leader must bring the purpose of work and the worker's purpose back into congruency by giving workers communal ownership of the organisation through justice and equitable distribution. He needs to:

* Institutionalise communication on the shop floor and at the interface
* Develop commonality of purpose by means of a clearcut philosophy
* Pursue the goals of the organisation singlemindedly.

In this manner, confidence and knowledge will be established by encouraging the worker to take the plunge rather than by trying to teach him how to swim on dry land.

Establish total cultural and worker involvement

A leader sees all the sub-elements in his organisation as belonging to one organisation. He must establish one cohesive team by not separating the sub-elements as if the brain can work without the heart. He needs to:

* Develop interdependence between the individual and the organisation
* Remove all trust barriers by showing trust
* Pursue participative involvement in all factors which affect the lives of the people

* Pursue joint decision-making by democratic vote for the liberation of initiative and creativity
* Bring distributive justice to all the stakeholders in the organisation.

By doing so, the worker's esteem and worth will be enhanced to the optimum. Productivity then becomes the major point of focus.

Improvement to process
* Managers seek solutions to problems. Leaders seek improvement to process.
* Managers do strategic things differently. Leaders do strategically different things.
* Out of this mindset, managers will try to sell "free enterprise" (effect), but leaders will conclude that it is not for sale until people are free to be enterprising (cause).
* A programme for black advancement (effect) will fail unless the culture of the organisation is conducive and non-hostile to the advancement of blacks (cause).
* Equal opportunity programmes (effect) will fail unless there is top commitment to establish equality in the organisation (cause).

Process translates into progress which in turn is also a dynamic element - non-measurable, no timetable and no absolute. To change process needs the changing of perception which in turn takes time. A leader needs to understand that the time dimension is a vital element in his formulation of strategy for the improvement of process which, by its very dynamic and changing nature, will only be manifested over a long period of time.

12/2:

16
Participative systems

To institutionalise participation as part of the business plan and the way of life of an organisation, it is necessary to establish a personalised system of interaction that will develop a communal ownership over the means of production, and evolve structures that will facilitate self-control in the workplace. Organisations that have achieved excellence through successful participative systems have usually also been innovative in developing unique and personalised options toward institutionalising participation and communication in the workplace.

What are the options?

Although the participative process does not always fit easily with traditional management methods and measurements, many organisations are talking about or embarking on implementing some system of participation. For some managers, the concept of participative systems is synonomous with the problem-solving teams known as quality circles, as implemented in Japan. This in itself is not a bad thing, but we must understand that quality circles as a form of participative management do have certain limitations and, although they have proved very successful in Japan and many other western organisations over the past thirty years, they may need to be further extended and personalised to address the challenges of South Africa today and in the future.

In his article on ''Revolt Against Working Smarter'' Bill Saporito makes the following observation on quality circles in western organisations:

> Quality circles, those hoola-hoops of 1980's management, are wobbling.
> The number of circles clocked by the international association of quality
> circles (IAQC) now exceeds 6 000, but growth proceeds by fits and starts,

with plenty of failures along the way .... The circles' proponents complain caustically that too many companies buy off-the-shelf programmes merely because everybody else has them, and then blame the consultants who help install them when the programmes fail. Without commitment from the top, goes the argument, even the best packages are doomed.

Too many organisations see quality circles, and other models, as an easy solution to the problems of productivity, quality and worker commitment. Rather than spend the time and energy on developing a personalised and unique system of participation for the business, management are often inclined to opt for ready-made, generic models of participative systems.

We are not suggesting that quality circles are ineffective, or the wrong way to go. We are saying, rather, that they are often incorrectly implemented and even where they are enjoying some degree of success, they may not necessarily be the best way to create pride, involvement and commitment among workers.

Many organisations attempting to implement quality circles, are meeting with resistance to the concept from unions and the workforce, who tend to see quality circles as yet another management ploy to exploit them. Cashbuild initially also experienced resistance - not because the system was bad, but simply because it was management-imposed and not worker designed. The CARE system was in fact incorrectly implemented, because neither the climate nor the culture was ready to accept it.

In fairness it must also be stated that this problem is not experienced by all organisations as much depends on the status of management/worker relationships and the entire culture within the organisation, as well as on variables outside the business.

A different problem with regard to quality circles is that they are inclined to address employee involvement only on the rational front of problem solving and suggestion making. Further commenting on resisting factors to quality circle implementation Saporito says:

> A bigger problem involved grievances. The company insisted that incidents on the shop floor such as reprimands and suspensions were not subjects for the circles to discuss. People are not faucets, they cannot be turned off emotionally. Says a local union president 'somebody on the shop floor gets disciplined and it creates emotion, and when that happens the company expects the people to go into quality circle meetings and forget what happened.'

In many instances, quality circles are implemented by management with the objective of getting workers to address quality and productivity problems, but without allowing them the right to address personal or communal issues which may indirectly be affecting their motivation and commitment to the organisation. By contrast Cashbuild, after four years of participative managment, is only now (1987) concentrating on the transfer of skills for solving problems which are work or product related.

Although there are some similarities between Cashbuild's VENTURECOMM system and quality circles, there are also major differences which are important to note if we are to understand the uniqueness of Cashbuild's system and some of the reasons why it has achieved such success.

The general structure and aim of quality circles

Quality circles are a means of providing employees with the opportunity to actively identify and resolve problems related to their work. It is a process in which management, salaried staff, hourly workers and where applicable unions, work together to jointly create a work climate where all employees can achieve work satisfaction by directing their ingenuity, imagination and creativity toward improving their work environment.

Operating teams are established to identify work related problems apart from their normal functional activities. Team leaders or facilitators are normally appointed and they guide the quality circle through a process of problem solving in order to analyse and recommend solutions for the day-to-day running activities of the business. Although some organisations try to enforce membership of quality circles, in most instances membership of quality teams is totally voluntary and no individual is requested or in any way pressurised to join a quality team.

Figure 25 indicates a typical quality circle operating process and its function within the organisation.

Quality circles are often the first major step towards meaningful worker participation in the decision-making process of a business. For many organisations they may be sufficient, serving to fulfil worker aspirations for many years and creating the type of involvement and commitment on the shop-floor that ensures excellence for the total organisation.

According to Saporito, however, quality circles initially:

> brightened the productivity landscape with a sort of giant Hawthorne effect: turn up the lights, productivity increases; turn down the lights, productivity increases - anything that suggests management cares. But the movement has done little to alter managerial behaviour in most companies. There is nothing wrong with a Hawthorne effect but it has to be distinguished from culture change. It was first generation: the second generation is really forcing companies to change in terms of the way they look at management's function. And there is the hitch.

150

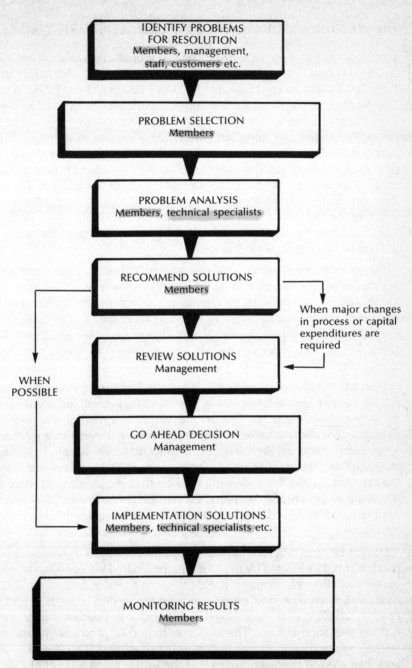

Figure 25: Generic model of the quality circle operating process

3)

The structure and function of Cashbuild's VENTURECOMM system

Cashbuild has broken away from the traditional management paradigm in creating its own, very different style of management. Up to middle management level there is no traditional form of managerial structure. A centralised form of managment, in which the department head would be making the majority, if not all, of the decisions and giving directives to the rest of his subordinates, has been supplanted by a system of managerial teams, which fulfil the traditional managerial role within every functional unit. In this team, the traditional manager retains the operations function which includes aspects such as budgeting, capital expenditure and land. The remaining managerial functions are, however, fulfilled by worker representatives who are elected by the workers and who, on an annual basis, hold portfolios of: quality of worklife, safety, labour, merchandising and whatever overall function is relevant to that unit.

All decisions pertaining to the operational activities of the functional unit are made by the relevant team of managers and workers. This group intrinsically serves as a balancing mechanism bridging the management and workers' viewpoints. All hard variable issues (profitability, expenditure, ROI's etc.) are discussed participatively and all soft variables (customer-service, stock, safety, employee needs, etc.) are managed through joint decision-making by vote.

The only constraint placed on this team is that they are discouraged from setting targets below those set by senior management unless it is for the purpose of building trust. This is an example of applying the "small win" principle that many excellent companies utilise in developing worker motivation. The team is, therefore, allowed to make decisions regarding outputs, quality, targets. In this way management and workers are participating at optimum levels. By allowing workers to participate and to share equitably in the success of the company, Cashbuild has discovered that employees are often inclined to set higher targets than management (and to achieve them).

It must be remembered that the VENTURECOMM system which consists of portfolio holders elected by the workers, originated via negotiation with employees at all levels through the CARE groups. As indicated earlier, these CARE groups consisted of groups of workers in different areas and levels of responsibility who were asked to identify any problems they had concerning the organisation. This was not limited to productivity and quality related issues. It was therefore through negotiation with the CARE groups and their elected representatives that the senior management of Cashbuild evolved the VENTURECOMM structure.

152

VENTURECOMM portfolio holders involve all members of the CARE groups in decisions made at VENTURECOMM meetings and, together with management, they communicate information regarding the hard variables which are the responsibility of the manager. Along with the VENTURECOMM system, CARE group meetings continue to be conducted to discuss problems, make suggestions or to resolve any issues that a worker may want to raise. The VENTURECOMM system is depicted in Figure 9 (p. 44).

The thorough-going process of negotiation carried out by Cashbuild again serves to emphasise the need to ensure that the philosophy of participation is first developed in the organisation before ventures of this nature are entered into. In the present Cashbuild system nothing is kept sacred from the employees any longer and the introduction of profit sharing signifies a

QUALITY CIRCLES	VENTURECOMM
1. Motivated and initiated by senior management to improve quality and productivity.	Motivated and initiated by senior management to develop human potential and dignity - quality and productivity are regarded as spinoffs.
2. Driven by management's focus on better "Return-on-Investment" through employee involvement.	Driven by a common management/worker focus on a philosophy based on human dignity (philosophy also developed jointly by all people in the business).
3. Allow workers the power to make suggestions and solve problems that are restricting quality and productivity. Management remain responsible for final decision-making and implementation.	Allows workers power over "soft variables" through joint decision-making with management. Workers are responsible and accountable through their elected portfolio members in VENTURECOMM.
4. Quality circles do not necessarily encourage involvement of workers in traditional mangerial responsibilities or "Holy Cows" such as capital expenditures.	VENTURECOMM insists on the sharing of information of the "hard variables". Managers remain responsible and accountable for aspects such as CAPEX but convey information and motives for decisions to VENTURECOMM.
5. Quality circles seldom involve all workers. More often quality circles will achieve around 20% involvement through voluntary affiliation.	VENTURECOMM aims to achieve 80-100% employee involvement.
6. Quality circles address rational problems with rational problem-solving techniques - this fits with a rational managerial process mindset (it does, however, not exclude a leadership/culture mindset).	VENTURECOMM addresses any issue that affects the people or the success of the business - this fits with a leadership process and mindset.
	continued

153

meaningful step towards realising the concept of every employee as an owner in the business.

VENTURECOMM is a system that has gone far beyond quality circles. For some it may be too risky and radical. Others may have introduced a personalised form of quality circles into their organisations and be experiencing success similar to that of VENTURECOMM. Other managers, the sceptics of human potential and dignity, will dismiss VENTURECOMM, quality circles or any other form of participation as ineffective, soft, or threatening to their own power base. To them we can only say: look at the bottom line results of the organisations that have such structures of participation. And look at the future macro environment in which your business will have to survive.

continued:

QUALITY CIRCLES	VENTURECOMM
7. Create an avenue for workers to communicate ideas and solutions for problems to management. Provide a forum for worker/management interaction.	Institutionalises communication, employee involvement and participation as a "way of life" in the business i.e. VENTURECOMM is more than just a problem-solving mechanism, it is all-embracing.
8. Aim at limited self-control and ownership over the means of production.	Aims at institutionalised self-control and ownership over the means of production. (Devolution of power from the top and empowerment from the bottom.)
9. Quality circles are structured to cope with the exceptions/problems i.e. peripheral aspects of the process of business on an intermittent basis.	Structured to ensure employee involvement and control over aspects concerning the process of business on an on-going basis.
10. Quality circles in many western organisations (unlike Japan) are implemented as a peripheral part of the total business plan or as an aspect of the human resources plan.	VENTURECOMM is an integrated, focal point of the total business plan.
11. In most companies, quality circles are designed to "fit in with" or complement the traditional or existing management structure.	Cashbuild's VENTURECOMM has negated the traditional structure up to middle management level and supplanted it with a system of teams of worker representatives with specific portfolios, who together with management fulfil the managerial role.

154

Lastly, some managers may be excited by the concept of VENTURECOMM and may want to transplant the structure into their own organisations as soon as possible. We hope they will not lose their enthusiasm but that they will also maintain their realism and accept that a sophisticated and institutionalised process of participation such as VENTURECOMM will take months and perhaps years to implement. Equally important - it must be modified and personalised until it suits the unique needs of the organisation concerned.

In conclusion, the points summarised in the table on pages 153 and 154 indicate the basic differences between quality circles and the VENTURECOMM system. The observations regarding quality circles are general and may not be relevant to organisations who have through their own innovation and commitment personalised and extended the functions of quality circles.

Observations regarding participative structures

In an assessment of participative systems, it becomes apparent that there are a variety of ideas and systems which could be implemented with results varying right across the spectrum of motivations from satisfying basic needs to creating the highest levels of feelings of self-esteem. The positivism, commitment and sense of involvement that these systems create undoubtedly make them a major priority for management. In the "Project Free Enterprise" investigation of working models of participative systems in over a hundred organisations, the following conclusions were reached:

* External culture plays no significant deterrent role. The corporate culture is the only variable that could prevent the successful implementation of participative systems.
* Managerial visibility and direct support of the system are of fundamental importance.
* There is no short, quick method of implementing participative systems. The VENTURECOMM systems have succeeded due to management's acceptance of multifaceted medium-term approaches over a period of several years.
* There may be a need to personalise systems but there is no significant need to customise them. This makes it extremely easy for South African companies to learn from South African experiences. Hopefully we will start looking inwards to our own successes rather than spending thousands of rands to visit Japan and the USA in order to rediscover our own actual solutions.
* In all instances of success, a process of starting small, ensuring success and then growing was followed.

155

* Participation in a group system must be voluntary at the lower levels of management and workers.
* It is necessary to include participative objectives in formal managerial and organisational objectives.
* Workers must be given the authority to implement solutions and investigate problems.
* Successes stemming from the participative system must be monitored and communicated with the maximum degree of exposure.
* It is necessary to ensure a basic understanding of the process of business, thereby instilling in the worker an acceptance of the fact that the quality of his own worklife is directly related to the outputs of the organisation, which in turn are dependent upon the quality and quantity of his own commitment, involvement and participation.

17
Reward systems

The success of participative systems and employee involvement in business is largely dependent on the development of an organic, performance-based (task) culture. The reward system and culture of an organisation are closely linked and thus have a profound influence on one another. It is unlikely that organisations will achieve meaningful participation and involvement from their workforce if they are not willing to be innovative in establishing reward systems that are commensurate with their people's efforts and aspirations. Quite simply you cannot expect excellence if you are not willing to reward excellence.

The status quo of reward systems in South Africa

For the vast majority of employees in South Africa there is little, if any, real correlation between their efforts and their rewards. Workers' perceptions that they are exploited by management are based on the reality of exploitation of the labour force in the past, the lack of employee participation in the success of a business and in decision-making and control over their own destiny, and many other factors which give the majority of workers no real vested interest in striving toward excellence.

Incentive reward systems have been identified as one of the major priorities for organisations to concentrate on at the micro level in order to survive the challenges of the future. Only by linking reward to levels of performance is it possible to develop the insight on the part of a worker that performance and the quality of labour inputs are important to *his* well-being, not just that of the organisation or the management.

An obstacle that management will encounter in the development of performance-based reward systems is the perception among workers that improvements in their financial rewards are more attributable to the interventions and pressure of the unions than on their own efforts in the workplace. It is also probable that organised labour will uphold the principle of equal pay for all jobs and reject differentiated pay, based on performance.

Management is largely to blame for this attitude of organised labour because it is management that has sliced organisations up into multitudes of layers in accordance with a variety of pay systems. These systems are inclined to classify people into boxes which prescribe their levels of responsibility and consequent rewards regardless of their individual performance. Unions have made the most of the situation by demanding across-the-board increases whereby all employees receive similar rewards regardless of the quality of their performance, whether mediocre or excellent.

The major problem experienced by organisations with rigid pay structures is that workers who are willing to increase standards of personal performance will do so only for a short period of time until they start recognising that their increased effort and performance are not justly rewarded. It is unfortunate but true that it is the lower level of performance that becomes the norm rather than the higher level of excellence. A worker whose performance is mediocre is not motivated to increase his personal contribution merely by the example of better performing colleagues; while the high-performance individual invariably becomes frustrated by the fact that his efforts are not being recognised and he then reduces his own output to the level of performance that is acceptable to management and on a par with his colleagues'.

Cashbuild's success in implementing effective participative systems has gone hand-in-hand with its ability to constantly expand its incentive reward systems in both monetary and non-monetary terms. Like other excellent organisations it has established systems to differentiate between different levels of performance, by recognising the contributions of individuals, teams and their systems as a whole.

Principles of performance-based reward systems

Debureaucratising

A fundamental principle of establishing a performance-based culture and an effective incentive reward system is to debureaucratise. It is necessary to get rid of all the rules, procedures and job descriptions which so often define and limit the parameters of an employee's contribution to the organisation. In essence, debureaucratising means a shift from a mechanistic/role culture toward one that is more organic/task orientated.

As has been pointed out earlier, these mechanistic/role cultures tend to offer the employee security and predictability; a constant rate of climb; reward for satisfactory rather than excellent performance; and dependence on organisational and managerial rather than individual capabilities.

158

Debureaucratising moves the organisation towards a more task-based culture where the emphasis is on getting the job done, rather than expending energy in adhering to rules and procedures. The task culture utilises the unifying power of the group to improve effectiveness and to identify the individual with the organisation's objectives. Decision-making is therefore contained in the group and individuals gain a high degree of control over their work.

By removing unnecessary rules and restrictions an organisation becomes more capable of being adaptable and sensitive to the dynamic challenges of the larger environment within which it has to operate.

Over the past few years Cashbuild has concentrated on ensuring that all employees are aware of the outputs expected from them as a team and as individuals. The focus has constantly been on living the organisation's philosophy, which is based on respect for human dignity and principles of excellence.

Cashbuild's approach to rules and job descriptions was clearly illustrated in Koopman's reply to a consultant who wanted to sell him a package of job descriptions and position charters. The consultant asked Koopman whether Cashbuild had job descriptions. Koopman replied "No we don't need them. The jobs people do define their job descriptions."

Rather than box people into rigid job descriptions, Cashbuild has given people the authority, responsibility and freedom to do what is necessary to achieve their objectives as a team, with minimum interference from management's side. This absence of rigid structure, rules and bureaucracy has not resulted in a chaotic or disorderly situation, but has rather freed the spirit of people to truly channel their energies towards performance levels of which they and the organisation can feel justly proud.

Self-control through negotiated target setting

Through the CARE and VENTURECOMM systems Cashbuild has given workers the power to negotiate with management on the setting of targets at their retail outlets. Although management makes decisions on budgets and the required return-on-investment to satisfy ongoing growth and shareholders' requirements, workers are involved in setting targets for their areas of responsibility. The VENTURECOMM team, consisting of management and elected workers, makes the necessary decisions related to the outputs, quality and targets that will ensure ongoing growth and wealth creation, from which all members of the business will benefit. The fact that management has entrusted workers with such high levels of responsibility has consistently resulted in the teams of workers setting realistic but challenging objectives.

The realistic principle of trusting people and allowing them to understand why they are performing activities and how these activities fit into the larger picture has resulted in a constant striving by the majority of the workforce towards ongoing improvements of quality, productivity and customer service. Most managers will admit that one of their most important rewards is their right to make decisions and to exercise control over their destiny. It is difficult to understand why they then fail to accept that people at the operational level also have these needs and will also experience these priviliges as rewards in themselves.

Cashbuild has also found that allowing people to do the job and to be involved in setting their own targets has developed mutual trust between management and the workers. Motivation to achieve also tends to become internalised and target achievement is self-enforced rather than externally driven by threats and policing by management.

Allowing self-control over targets and the creation of wealth is an important step towards creating an atmosphere where people want to perform because it restores their pride and allows them the dignity of getting credit for the success of their work.

"Small wins" and achievability

For reward systems to be effectively linked to performance it is important that people should be managed in such a way that they are encouraged to perform. Performance management is founded on the basic principle that behaviour is a result of action. This implies that a person's job performance can be changed by changing what happens to that person as a result of his or her performance. Therefore, if the consequences are favourable, the employee continues to perform at the same level, or better: if the consequences are unfavourable, he or she will decrease the effort or cease it all together.

In certain instances, Cashbuild has opted for setting a slightly lower target in order to produce a positive consequence for the team that achieves their target, rather than setting a high, unreachable target that results in a feeling of a failure. In *Pursuit of Excellence*, Peters and Waterman also indicated that excellent companies were inclined to concentrate on the "small win" and on ensuring positive consequences in the thousand and one little things that employees did every day. In most organisations however, managers fail to relate consequences directly to individual or team performance and although they give salary increases, bonuses and even profit sharing, employees see no direct correlation between their efforts and the rewards they are offered. At Cashbuild, the VENTURECOMM system has ensured that individuals and teams are consistently made aware of the impact of their behaviour on the success of the business.

160

Developmental versus judgemental focus

Reward systems in many organisations are determined by performance appraisals, in which managers judge an employee's performance over a period of a year and give merit increases accordingly. Most of the systems seem to become judgemental and the employee feels threatened and defensive about his or her behaviour. This leads to the common situation in which employees feel victimised because a manager focuses his appraisal on the things they did wrong during the course of the year so that he can contain the merit increases at the lowest possible level and in the process meet his budget constraints. The result of this is that employees are often afraid to make mistakes or are inclined to hide errors from management for fear of the dreaded performance appraisal. This stifles initiative and reaffirms the employee's perception that, regardless of performance, the appraisal will ensure that he will end up with the same across-the-board increase that everybody else gets.

Cashbuild's willingness to allow employees to be involved in setting targets and their encouragement of innovation and contribution by the workforce, and its acceptance that errors might occur, ensure that workers feel that the emphasis in the business is developmental rather than judgemental. Cashbuild does not ignore errors or fail to reprimand poor work performance but is more inclined to concentrate on the winning behaviour and on providing positive consequences for positive contributions.

It must also be noted that the ability to maintain a developmental rather than a judgemental focus is highly dependent on a specific manager's ability and style within any given department or area of the business. It is unlikely that this aspect of the reward system will be consistently handled throughout any organisation due to the different styles and backgrounds of various managers who may still believe that paying a worker at the end of the month is reward enough and that it is unnecessary to spend effort or energy on consistently ensuring that workers experience positive consequences from their efforts. In excellent companies, however, managers are inclined to change their styles as the culture shifts and as they see the results their colleagues are achieving through effective performance management and application of the principle of ''small wins''.

Team versus individual reward

The western ideal of rewarding only individual performance, creates a variety of problems. For many employees it is unacceptable that they should be distinguished and singled out from their peers for their individual performance. In the South African context this often means that they will be seen as siding with management and consequently siding against their fellow workers.

161

Rather than seeing this need for collective identification as a hurdle, Cashbuild has utilised it as a major source of energy. A significantly large proportion of employees prefer to stand out inside the crowd rather than to stand out from the crowd. It therefore made sense to allow people to strive for incentives and improved rewards as a team rather than as individuals. This does not negate the fact that people are individuals or that they have unique needs and aspirations, it merely states that these unique needs and aspirations may be easier to achieve within the collective effort of a group or team. Cashbuild's reward systems are therefore geared to rewarding team achievements whilst also rewarding individual contributions to the improvement of the functioning of the team as a whole. In this way poor and mediocre performers are encouraged to raise their standards, in contrast with the situation where high performers lower their standards so as to maintain their identification with the group.

Rewards are given to the team for activities such as sytems improvement and debureaucratising, reduction of shrinkage and waste, increase of sales etc. These rewards are also passed onto the system as a whole in terms of the success of the entire business, which encourages cooperation between various departments and business units.

Although Cashbuild concentrates on developing winning teams and establishing team effort, it also encourages individual growth through various systems of succession planning. Positive behaviour displaying a concern for the company as an economic unit by any individual is also rewarded, and this is found to be totally acceptable to the workforce in general because it shows a concern for the team rather than for personal benefits only.

An example of this type of reward for individual innovation, was the large bonus given to an employee for his efforts in helping avert a shopping boycott of Cashbuild's stores in a specific region. On his own initiative he negotiated with the groups that were calling for a general boycott of all white businesses and he was able to demonstrate to them that Cashbuild had the interests of all its employees at heart, both black and white, and that black employees were treated with dignity, respect and fairness. This resulted in Cashbuild being able to continue its business while many others were brought to a standstill. This action indicated a concern for the safety of fellow workers and for their need to maintain their livelihood, and was generously rewarded as such.

Creation of wealth and equitability in the distribution of wealth

Through the VENTURECOMM system, Cashbuild allows employees to make operational decisions in concert with management that to a large extent determine the success and profitability of the business. The fact that workers

162

participate so fully and democratically in the business means that they contribute very directly to the creation of wealth within the business, and Cashbuild therefore feels that it is just and correct that they should participate in the distribution of this wealth as they do in all other facets of the business. Many organisations have been unable to establish worker participation and commitment for the very reason that they have expected workers to help in the creation of wealth, but failed to allow them to benefit from the distribution of wealth.

It must be understood that Cashbuild's philosophy has always been that prior to equality in distribution of wealth, opportunities had to be equalised. This means that through the effective involvement of workers in the process of the business, additional wealth is created and workers are seen to be justly deserving of sharing this increased wealth with the shareholders.

Rewards for aspects of the job over which the worker has control

A simple and rather obvious principle of effective incentive reward systems is that workers should be rewarded for contributions over which they have control. In many organisations the profit sharing or incentive schemes tend to include activities and parameters over which the workers have absolutely no control. This necessarily causes demotivation as workers feel that regardless of their efforts they may be punished or not properly rewarded for their contributions due to their failures in activities over which they have no authority and no involvement.

Establishing credibility with organised labour

The perception exists that organised labour will resist any incentive reward system. Although this perception may be accurate in certain instances, it is more likely that organised labour is resistant to incentive reward systems because it questions management's objectivity in the application of such schemes and it frankly does not have any historical reason to believe that management is willing to "share the loot".

Cashbuild has managed to establish a performance-based culture and to implement incentive reward systems with very little resistance from any unions. In fact, unions were supportive of these actions once they saw that management's intentions were honest and that they were willing to match their words with deeds.

Given the fact that unions are here to stay and that they are an integral part of the business system, it is essential that management should invest a great deal of effort in negotiating with and involving organised labour in the development of performance-based cultures which differentially reward enhanced performance. This would certainly be to the benefit of all parties concerned.

Methods of reward

It is impossible to prescribe generic methods of reward that would enable all organisations to elicit participation and commitment from their workforce. At best we can indicate some examples of methods used in Cashbuild and other organisations which may stimulate ideas, or be adapted for use by an organisation embarking on transformation towards a more participative system.

A fundamental principle to be adhered to in applying any method of reward is that the environment must be prepared and ready to accept it. Many organisations have embarked on admirable reward schemes such as profit participation and shareholding for their workers before ensuring that workers were actually participating in the process of the business. In the South African context many black, "Asian" and coloured workers will not be motivated by profit participation or shareholding while they perceive the system to be unjust. The view of many workers and unions is that they would be condoning injustice and exploitation if they participated in profit sharing and shareholding in a business which does not practise meaningful employee involvement, equality for all people, justice, and recognition of human dignity. Cashbuild embarked on profit sharing only after four years of employee involvement through the VENTURECOMM system. Open communication was institutionalised and democracy, justice and trust were established before true profit participation was implemented. We cannot emphasise this point too strongly, because it is inherent in the worker's motivation to seek justice or dignity prior to adjusting the effects of his productivity or labour.

The rule is quite simple. Do not implement incentive reward systems in an organisation or culture where employees have no understanding of the process of business or method of influencing the means of production. Certainly they will accept management's hand-out of profits but without really becoming more committed or motivated to improve their performance, because a lack of trust and involvement will still govern their actions.

Preparation of an environment that will accept a performance-based reward system is essential and the following monetary and nonmonetary methods of reward may give some guidelines for implementation.

Sharing of shrinkage savings

Cashbuild has implemented a monetary incentive for employees to reduce waste and shrinkage. A specific, acceptable percentage is budgeted for stock

164

loss and waste. This may, for example, be determined at 1% of total turnover in a retail environment. <u>Employees are then encouraged to maintain shrinkage or waste figures below 1% and they are given whatever is saved.</u> If a branch is turning over one million rand per year, a 1% budget per year on waste will amount to R10 000. If employees are, in fact, able to reduce the waste or shrinkage figure to 0,5%, they will be given the R5 000 which has been saved.

This system is obviously flexible and needs to be adapted to the requirements of a given organisation. It is essential, however, that the <u>organisation should have effective methods of measuring waste or shrinkage</u> to ensure fair distribution of the reward. In a production environment it would obviously be essential that <u>effective quality control</u> is implemented to ensure that waste figures are not kept artificially low by simply passing substandard products on to the consumer. This system of sharing the saving on waste or shrinkage helps employees to understand the process of business better and ensures ongoing quality and productivity in their work. It also gives the organisation the opportunity to reward an entire branch or team for its efforts, rather than only the high performing individual.

Share allocation

Many organisations allocate shares to their employees as a means of creating a vested interest in the success of the business. Cashbuild has implemented a system whereby employees can acquire shares at preferential rates, <u>depending on their length of service, level of responsibility or contribution to the organisation.</u> It is important to note that Cashbuild first created a high level of trust and commitment between management and employees before offering these shares to its people. This enabled employees to accept or strive towards share-holding in the organisation without feeling that this would put them in the position of siding with a system or a structure with which they disagreed.

Profit sharing

The article published in the *Financial Times* (August 23 1985) from which we quote below is an example of an ingenious pay formula, which gives employees a fair share of the corporate cake. This formula may not be applicable in all organisations but it does give some idea of the kind of innovations a management team could implement.

> There is a company in the south-east of England which can lay claim to not having given its employees a pay rise for over 10 years. Perhaps

more remarkable is that it is over 20 years since its employees have asked for one.

The company is not, however, some autocratic sweatshop left over from Dickensian times. Far from it: Its employees have an unusual degree of freedom to control their own working lives and enjoy considerably higher incomes than people in comparable jobs. This state of affairs has been brought about through the adoption of an ingenious management system which has the twin advantages of keeping the company costs rigidly under control while guaranteeing its employees a share in its growth.

The company is Southern Business Leasing, a Croydon-based organisation with 158 employees and agents, a turnover of £6,1m and a quotation on the unlisted securities market. Its business is renting out and servicing Canon Photocopiers and Maxpax drink vending machines - mainly the former - throughout the South East.

Its management system was introduced by George Stewart, the chairman, and implemented by David McErlain, the managing director. The concept is simple. Total turnover is seen as a cake divided into slices. A 25% slice goes immediately to profit and the rest is used to cover the company's costs.

The biggest slice - 30% of turnover - is used to cover the cost of sales, consisting mainly of the amortisation of machines and the cost of consumables such as ink and paper.

The rest of the cake is allocated to the company's operating divisions. Servicing gets 16%, sales 9%, establishment (telephone, rates, insurance) 7%, administration 6%, finance 5% and distribution 2%.

At the end of each quarter the company calculates the turnover for the period and divides it according to the percentage laid down. At the same time each operating division's costs for the period are calculated and set against the amount it is due to receive. The balance - and this is the key element of the system - is not retained by the company but goes directly to that division's employees in the form of a quarterly bonus.

...The advantage for the company lies in better financial control. Says McErlain: "It takes away that dread which every manager has that overheads are growing as a proportion of turnover. It just can't happen in this company because the overheads are completely self-regulating".

Another advantage is that the annual squabble over pay rises is eliminated. The company avoids the risk of losing employees through paying them too little and at the same time knows it is not paying them more than it can afford.

From the employees' point of view, their guaranteed share in the growth of the company has increased their pay much more quickly than they could hope to have seen through annual pay negotiation. For example, they say, their service engineers are earning about £20 000 a year against perhaps £10 000 elsewhere in the industry. There are no trade union members at Southern.

166

Nonmonetary methods of reward

Creating a performance-based culture and an effective reward system is also dependent on implementing certain nonmonetary rewards which make people feel that the standard of their performance (excellent *or* inadequate) is being acknowledged.

At Cashbuild, Koopman introduced a system of what he called "Albert the Lion Letters". These might compliment employees on little things that they had done which indicated a concern and striving towards excellence. They could also be written to reprimand an employee who was not performing according to his or her full potential.

Personal communication from senior executives in the organisation gives employees a sense that management is in touch with them and whether the notes are complimentary or reprimanding, employees still feel motivated because they see a direct link between their behaviour and the consequences of that behaviour.

Another method of nonmonetary reward used by Cashbuild, applies to an employee working on a corporate project. The employee is flown up from his branch to the head office to participate in a management workshop relating to the project. It is incredible what levels of motivation and feelings of reward an employee experiences when he sees that management respects him sufficiently to go to these lengths and to this expense.

Yet another method of reward in Cashbuild is the distribution of merit certificates for excellent performance by an individual or team. These certificates are handed out by senior management at meetings of the entire staff. This is obviously a form of recognition for excellent performance and again gives employees a feeling of belonging and the knowledge that their behaviour is being linked to successful consequences in the business.

Cashbuild also conducts national indabas or meetings at which members of VENTURECOMM groups are brought together for week-long conferences to discuss all aspects of the business and any ideas or concerns for the future. Once again this method shows employees that their opinions are important because management is consulting direct with their elected representatives and involving them with the ongoing running of the organisation.

Iscor is another organisation which has introduced nonmonetary rewards. It has implemented a system whereby competitions are run for their Omega quality circle groups. In this process the total commitment of management to recognising employee involvement is made very apparent. Participating groups go through a series of preliminary rounds until a few teams ultimately qualify for the national final. Several hundred managers and their partners are invited to this function to listen to the presentations of the teams. Chief executive officers, general managers and previous team members sit on a panel to assess the winning teams, and the entire emphasis is on the recognition of the teams' efforts and their achievements. The climate that this creates among workers can best be illustrated by a comment made by one of the 1985 finalists: "When I started my work I did not know exactly what was expected of me. I was a little dumb. Then I heard about Omega and joined this team. Now I understand my job and know exactly what management wants from me and that management listens to me." This type of interaction with management is rewarding to the worker who feels that he is being recognised for his individual and team contribution.

Many other monetary and nonmonetary reward systems can be developed. Different organisations need to find specific formulae according to their own specific cultures and environments. The important thing is that these rewards should indicate to <u>employees</u> that the <u>consequences of their actions</u> are <u>directly linked to the rewards that they will receive.</u>

To develop such unique options in an organisation, management may be well advised to follow the participation route and to ask workers what they would perceive as a fair and just reward system, rather than going the traditional route of deciding what would be best for workers and autocratically imposing these systems on them.

18
Democracy in the workplace

Losing control

For many managers, to allow participation by the workforce is to lose power and control. This is perhaps a natural fear in corporations which have been specifically structured in such a way as to entrench management's "right to control". This right to control is protected through a multitude of manuals, rules and the efficiency of doing things right. Managers become risk-averse entrepreneurs who protect their own and the shareholders' interests by maintaining total control over the means of production and the access to power. The employee becomes an executor of functions within a narrow and well-defined set of rules and regulations. He is not expected to think but rather to do his job as expected and be thankful for the security which the organisation offers him in wages and benefits.

Drucker's (1985) words provide a perfect focus regarding this issue:

> He (the employee) is paid, paid well in fact, much too well for the amount of responsibility demanded of him .... And that, at bottom, explains his unease, discontent, his psychological hollowness. Today's employee has income and income security. He has power in political society but lacks power in his own institution. He has function but lacks status. He lacks responsibility.

In the South African context the vast majority of people do not even have power in the political domain. The black worker not only lacks power in his own institution but also lacks power in society. This reduces even further his sense of purpose.

These circumstances tend to create disparities between the organisation and the individual. These disparities, unless addressed, negate meaningful participation in and commitment by all employees to the success of the business.

169

And such a situation, unless it is itself addressed, threatens the very existence of the business. In the United States, the threat is, by and large, that Japanese businesses are showing that they can consistently outdo American corporations in terms of price, quality, output, delivery dates and the like. In this part of the world, the threat is that the free enterprise system itself will fail to capture the commitment of working people as a group, and will accordingly cease to exist.

Our response to the fear that managers will lose control is therefore, in the first instance, to suggest that these managers may find themselves without any organisation over which control can be exercised.

Secondly, we ask them to examine a little more closely the righteousness of their position regarding control. The purpose of a business organisation, ultimately, is to generate profits. The organisation and its systems do not, in fact, exist for the purpose of protecting the right to control of any of its members. What the organisation requires of its management team is to fulful the ultimate purpose of the organisation, by whatever means will achieve this. Once this is accepted, a manager can free himself of the need to control, and can engage in the far more creative activity of shaping a committed team capable of exercising self-control in order to achieve its (shared) goals. Such a manager is unlikely to lose his place in the organisation, to become redundant or be bypassed.

Participation and socialism

The implementation of a democratic decision-making system such as Cashbuild's VENTURECOMM is seen by many as leaning towards socialism at the expense of shareholders and management.

By now it will be clear that the tenor of the many arguments in support of participation which we have quoted and referred to, is that corporate survival, health and growth depend on the introduction of democracy and participation in the work environment. A decision not to budge from the autocratic, mechanistic traditions is, in fact, a decision that is taken at the expense of shareholders and management.

The whole point of the corporate crusade for democracy and participation is that this is what will circumvent the demise, not only of the individual corporation, but of the free enterprise system as a whole. Perputation of the free enterprise system is most certainly not one of the aims of socialism.

Towards a new vision

For far too long the excessive bureaucratic rules of organisations have destroyed individual creativity and initiative. And for far too long business has suffered the consequence of low productivity as a result of these rules. The

170

blame for low productivity has more often than not been placed squarely in the court of the worker.

In order to separate symptom (worker performance) from real cause (organisational inadequacies), the organisational system needs to be reviewed. This section seeks to explore the necessity of moving beyond the confines of capitalism vs. socialism toward a system of principled pragmatism enabling business to survive the challenges of a turbulent macro environment.

New economic aims for the organisation should include:

* Allowing initiative on the part of the worker in contributing to technical and process improvements
* Reinstating distributive justice
* Offering security against destitution and exploitation
* Liberating creative forces for active participation and meaningful contribution.

If we pursue these aims, and focus on the worth of the worker, the fortunes of the organisation as an economic unit will change dramatically. Commonality of purpose becomes the driving force in the reference framework of both management and the workforce.

One might argue that points two and three are socialistic, and feel uncomfortable with them, but they are absolutely essential if points one and four are to be achieved. The problem with the system at large is that neither capitalism nor socialism actually allows the individual worker expression in the workplace.

To merely replace a driving capitalist or captain of industry, with all the perceived exploitative practices that accompany his style, with a socialistic bureaucrat who is an inherent overregulator, serves no purpose for either productivity or the lot of man. By and large, neither of them really welcomes initiative from the shopfloor.

One might argue that improvement of wages and working conditions is the proof of the need for their existence (which it might be), but surely if the economic aims, as put forward earlier, are practised and institutionalised within organisations then justice must prevail in the exchange of labour for goods. In order to achieve these aims the following two points of focus are paramount:

* Devolution of power from the top
* Empowerment from the bottom.

Management and labour need to have a common focus, so that the purpose of work and the worker's purpose become inseparable. Structures

171

which are to emerge should be between the organisation and individual and not between management and labour. Leadership principles which focus on the ultimate mission of the organisation need to harmonise with employee participation. This creates the synergistic effect in which the worker's purpose and the purpose of the organisation work hand in hand for the common good for all.

This objective can best be achieved by creating a set of criteria on which employee performance can be judged and suitably rewarded. A sense of communal ownership over part of the means of production is absolutely vital in creating substantial organisational commitment.

Surely the usefulness of work, dignity and self-respect, can only be achieved through a true democratic right to have a say in one's destiny. This is the least that can be done to restore pride in order to gain commitment. In Cashbuild, true democracy is now expressed as participative democracy and not representative democracy. To restore the esteem and worth of the worker he must be able to express a choice regarding the selection of his immediate leader/manager and be able to remove him if unsuitable. This is participative democracy in its purest form. It is also not surprising that, given management's negative perceptions of the workforce, they cringe at the thought of allowing workers such levels of power. The fascinating reality is that in Cashbuild over the past few years, these fears and perceptions have proved to be largely unfounded. Only two managers have been fired by the workforce using the VENTURECOMM mechanism. In both cases the managers were blatantly guilty of grossly infringing the basic philosophy of the business. In the one case, the manager was consistently racist towards both employees and customers. This was totally unacceptable since it violated the principle of respect for human dignity and the belief in the worth of both customer and employee. In the other case, the manager was dismissed for theft. Such dishonesty obviously infringed the rights of the employees, the management and the company. These examples tend to make nonsense of the popular assumption that the workers will immediately abuse delegated power and responsibility. On the contrary, the employees of Cashbuild have displayed remarkable responsibility in the use of the power and trust placed in them.

With the implementation of a participative democracy the unfair power balance of the typical management-labour relationship is replaced with a more equitable power balance between organisation and individual.

The "usefulness of work" on the part of the salary/wage earner and the "right to control the workplace" by the organisation, thus take on a common focus. The business can therefore focus singlemindedly on its prime purpose - to create wealth for the good of all its stakeholders.

To many this may sound too radical a departure from traditional management practice. Drucker, regarded as one of the world's most eminent management visionaries, spells out this philsophy in his *Managing in Turbulent Times:*

> If the employee/owner can be integrated into the power process and mobilised to support the enterprise, management will again have a ground of legitimacy. It will again have a power base. There will again be a constituency for the producer interest in society, and the employee for whose benefit business is mainly run in his dual capacity as holder of a job and as beneficial owner. But this cannot happen automatically. It requires that employees, both as owners of society's capital and as possessors of society's knowledge be endowed with responsibility.
>
> Management's job is to make human strength more productive. The shift of knowledge to the worker and the steady upgrading of competence in the workforce represents a very large, almost unprecedented increase in the potential of human strength in the developed countries. It is in fact what makes them developed. Yet by and large, managements in developed countries have not taken the initiative in converting this potential of strength into the actual of responsibility of citizenship. Managers have as a rule failed to take the initiative, failed to take advantage of the tremendous opportunity that the shift from the proletarian represents, and have thus not made fully productive the resources in their keeping. The employee in most companies, and even more in most public service institutions, is basically underemployed. His responsibility does not match his capacity, his authority and his economic position. He is given money instead of the status that only general responsibility can confer - and this is a trade-off that never works. Specifically, the employee on all levels from the lowest to the highest needs to be given genuine responsibility ... he must be held responsible for setting the goals for his own work and for managing himself by objectives and self-control. He must be held responsible for the constant improvement of the entire operation - what the Japanese call continuous learning. He must share responsibility in thinking through and setting the enterprise's goals and objectives, and in making the enterprise's decisions.
>
> This is not democracy, it is citizenship. It is not being permissive. It is also not merely "participative management" - which is often only a futile attempt to disguise the reality of employee impotence through psychological manipulation. Actually imposing responsibility on the employees - for plant community affairs; for their own goals and objectives; for continuous improvement in the performance of their own work and job - immeasurably strengthens management in the same way in which decentralisation in the multi-divisional company always strengthens management. It creates a better understanding of management decisions and managerial attitudes throughout the workforce (Drucker, 1985).

173

Drucker here advocates that businesses that wish to survive turbulence and meet the challenge of the future should ensure more than the nominal participation of their workforce. He is advocating communal ownership over the means of production and the evolution of democratic structures directed towards self-control. This means more than the implementation of quality circles or suchlike processes.

Cashbuild's VENTURECOMM system of participative democracy surpasses the traditional western forms of participative management and participative systems. It allows citizenship for all its people in the business. This is best reflected in the main objective of VENTURECOMM:

> VENTURECOMM will serve as a platform for freedom of speech and upward mobility of staff and for the active involvement of all races, religions, sexes and creeds in the day-to-day running of a Cashbuild branch. It will serve through a process of joint decision-making and participative management to involve people at all levels in the running of the business. Effective communication and time management thus achieved will lead to an era of trust building by virtue of developing unparalleled company commitment through direct team effort and company shared values (VENTURECOMM Creed of Trust).

The Cashbuild VENTURECOMM system therefore addresses socialism on two fronts, reinstating distributive justice and offering security against destitution. It addresses capitalism in the manner that true expression is given to reward and effort. As the worker becomes more productive, so the organisation becomes more profitable. Commensurate with this increase in productivity, the worker shares in greater rewards via the profit-sharing scheme. The benefits to all the stakeholders is more than obvious. This is principled pragmatism in practice.

Most significantly however, this system liberates the worker from fear by virtue of its underlying democratic principles. Fear is replaced by hope - the hope of a better life through a common vision shared by all. VENTURECOMM gives expression to the work ethic and spirit of man.

True participation by all the people in the business through the development of communal ownership over the means of production and the evolution of democratic structures for self-control, is a process and not a single act. In Cashbuild the evolution of this process took more than two years - and that in a business where the executive regarded participation as among its highest strategic priorities. Impatient premature movement towards such communal ownership and democratic structures, without the necessary preparation of the micro environment, will be doomed to failure. The process is evolutionary by nature.

174

Creativity through participation

In examining the performance of the Cashbuild business over a number of years, Koopman came to the conclusion that a greater number of people had left the organisation as a result of boredom than because of overwork. From the interviews he held with his staff, it became apparent that too many of the jobs in the organisation were totally denuded of responsibility and hence provided little or no interest for the people who occupied them.

Productivity comes essentially from committed people whose perceptions about their jobs are positive. Rigid job descriptions, over-control, and negative motivation result in non-performance from employees. Through institutionalising participative democracy Cashbuild experienced the following visible impacts on productivity.

* Allowing initiative: Workshops attended by the people who actually do the work have redesigned Cashbuild's entire creditor system, achieving an annual saving of well over R200 000 per annum.
* Distributive justice: By introducing profit sharing for all, Cashbuild has realigned its corporate purpose along the lines of overall wealth creation. Despite having distributed some 12,5% of net profit before tax to workers, the additional wealth created for the organisation was 29%.
* Offering security against destitution: The drop in staff turnover from 126% in 1982 to 9% in 1986 brought about significant savings in the form of training and other employment costs and a corresponding increase in bottom-line contribution.
* Liberating creativity: By allowing people a say over the workplace, and allowing them to make mistakes, Cashbuild has:
  • Built up a significant number of future managers within its ranks.
  • Dispersed trade knowledge of the basic business function to a greater number of people in the business. (More people understand the basics of the business and are able to contribute toward its success.)
  • Redesigned the entire organisation with a subsequent improvement in responsibility and accountability.
  • Allowed a new and more visionary business strategy to flow from this culture of liberated creative forces.

In anyone's language, this all adds up to productivity!

13/2

19
Overview

It is more than apparent that the results of the Cashbuild philosophy have been very substantial indeed. An ongoing analysis of the profit and earnings yield figures confirm emphatically that people who become committed to the corporate crusade are individuals who make organisational effectiveness a way of life. They are the ones who take it upon themselves to protect the organisation against the onslaught from its competitors. These are the same individuals who become responsible for buttoning down corporate efficiency. In short, people who make the major difference to corporate excellence are the employees themselves. They are the cornerstones on which the organisation is built. The extra mile, as described in the Cashbuild approach, can only be achieved through optimal employee involvement and commitment. In this respect the Cashbuild approach has revolutionised management thinking in South Africa. The degree to which perceptions at Cashbuild have changed is more than obvious, not only from the discussion in the previous chapters, but also in the level of commitment, reflected in the turn-around of corporate financial results. Freedom to perceive the organisation as a caring family in which dignity and justice are the order of the day, breeds a sense of crusading loyalty which is unparalleled in other organisational models.

A new corporate vision
The key to success in the Cashbuild story is liberation - the liberation of both management and employees' perceptions about the organisation and what it stands for. This liberation has taken place as a result of the development of trust, shared power, freeing of creativity, attention to human dignity, genuine participative management, and inclusion of everyone in the larger corporate family.

In Cashbuild, management realised that for attitudes to become positive and permanent the focus had to be on an internal locus of control. It was

176

imperative that employees became masters of their own destiny within the parameters of the greater Cashbuild organisation. People who are permitted to exercise self-control make things happen even when there are many obstacles in the pathway to goal achievement. For them it is important to eliminate obstacles which interfere with the satisfaction that will be derived from such goal attainment. Unlike externally motivated people, they do not depend on structures and centralisation or intervention to achieve corporate results.

The perceptions which have emerged from this corporate transformation process indicate that an environment in which the basic tenets of entrepreneurship apply - in the sense of liberating creativity via fundamental risk taking - is enormously rewarding. The message is really very simple. People will tend to respond when given the challenge. The assumption is that employees have a great deal of stretch to offer the corporation in terms of their talent and basic energy. When this extra stretch is made available to the corporation by committed employees, the outcome, in terms of the hard measurements such as yield, growth, profits and ongoing return-on-assets managed, is substantial. Cashbuild's balance sheets bear witness to this in a most emphatic manner.

From grey to defined roles

One of the fundamental strengths of the Cashbuild philosophy was that it looked at the workers' needs in matching man and organisation. The basic belief was that via maximum devolution of power, employees would be able to satisfy many of their inherent needs within the context of corporate life. This would mean that much of the energy which would otherwise be diverted to activities outside of the organisational needs, would become focused on specific corporate objectives. The bottom line contribution is more than apparent from the results reported in this study.

The traditional concepts of job descriptions and ongoing job appraisals were replaced by a notion that employees would define their own roles if given the opportunity to do so. More importantly, there would be a synergy among these roles in the corporate environment to the benefit of the corporate objective. Again, the results have indicated beyond all reasonable doubt that this has been the case. Far fom dodging individual responsibilities, employees have become more productive and far more corporate-centered than previously.

The management of corporate change

In the establishment of both VENTURECOMM and the CARE groups, the demand was for employee-centred leadership. Such leadership did, in fact, emerge and sustained itself on a growing sense of trust between management and the workforce in the Cashbuild operation. The removal of various artificial barriers proved to be most sensible. Ongoing demand for reviewing the management practices on such issues as job structures, performance appraisals, and reward systems is more than apparent. The fundamentals of organic management demand this as part of the formula for ensuring healthy progressive change.

Summary

In conclusion it must be said that what has been learnt from the Cashbuild analysis is that management is involved in an ongoing search for solutions which create more effective and efficient organisations. It projects a message of continuing evolution and a need for constant flexibility in the way organisations conduct themselves. There can be no doubt that the results from such an approach will pay enormous dividends well into the future.

Visionary management is the major variable on which Cashbuild has built its success story. The components of visionary management have been analysed. Therefore let it suffice to say that calculated risk taking and the freeing of creativity are major dimensions in the contribution to corporate excellence. The crusade for excellence continues. The corporate army marches on.

not just putting fires out but better performance

13/2

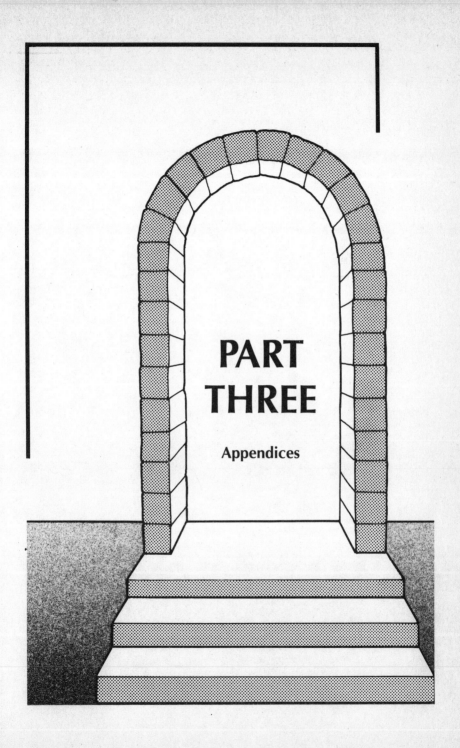

PART THREE

Appendices

APPENDIX 1

The Cashbuild VENTURECOMM Creed of Trust

Creed of Trust
of the
CASHBUILD VENTURECOMM
ideal

1. AIM

Venturecomm will serve as a platform for freedom of speech and upward mobility of staff and for the active involvement of all races, religions, sexes and creeds in the (day-to-day) running of a Cashbuild Branch. It will serve as a platform for genuine management involvement by all staff through a process of joint decision-making and participative management at all levels. Effective communication and time management thus achieved will lead to an era of trust building by virtue of developing unparalleled company commitment through directed team effort and shared company values

2. INTERPRETATION

2.1   The "Philosophy" shall mean CARE Plan as set out in our booklet of shared values as to why we do certain things the way we do at Cashbuild.

Culture

2.2   "Management" shall mean the collective body of VENTURECOMM and its Office Bearers.

2.3   The "Organisation" shall mean the greater order to which all consideration has to be given in determining decisions based on "the greater good for the greater whole" within the framework of its philosophy and manual.

2.4 The "Executive" shall mean that body of operational line managers directly responsible for the overall control of the organisation, e.g. General Manager, Operations Manager and Personnel Manager.

3. MEMBERSHIP

3.1 Number

VENTURECOMM will consist of five members (Office Bearers) ideally. There may not be an equal number of people. In smaller branches Portfolios will have to overlap.

3.2 Portfolios

3.2.1 Portfolios are specific areas of responsibility which Office Bearers will control and be held responsible for. Powers and authority over these areas will be clarified in point 5.

3.2.2 The five main Portfolios will be:

* Operations
* Labour
* Safety
* Quality of Worklife
* Merchandising

3.3 Elections and requirements for election

A) Members

3.3.1 Our current Presidents of CARE Group I and CARE Group II as well as the Branch Manager will automatically become members of VENTURECOMM.

3.3.2 The remaining two/three members are to be elected by secret ballot voting but before putting themselves up for election, they <u>must show that they have the necessary knowledge and skills to cope</u> with the demands of their Portfolios.

3.3.3 Elections are to be held during normal working hours at a time agreed to by the Manager and Presidents to elect the VENTURECOMM members.

3.3.4 It is the branch's choice to let current Presidents for CARE Group I and CARE Group II retain their titles and responsibilities for their respective Groups as well as being members of VENTURECOMM.

B) Chairman and Vice-chairman

3.3.5 VENTURECOMM members will, by a show of hands, elect a Chairman and Vice-chairman on a monthly rota basis.

3.3.6 VENTURECOMM members may make themselves available for <u>Chairman and Vice-chairman.</u>

C) Term of office

3.3.7 VENTURECOMM members are generally elected for one year at the Annual General Meeting.

3.3.8 <u>A VENTURECOMM member shall cease to hold office as such, if he/she fails to attend three successive meetings, unless it is resolved by the VENTURECOMM members prior to the 3rd meeting that he should remain in office.</u>

3.3.9   A VENTURECOMM member has the right to resign
        by giving 14 days' written notice to the Chairman or
        if the Chairman is the resigning person, to the
        Vice-chairman.

3.3.10 The VENTURECOMM management team shall have
        the right to co-opt persons to serve thereon, either in
        the place of a VENTURECOMM member who has
        ceased to hold office or as an additional member (in
        the case of bigger branches). Such co-opted member
        will serve until the next Annual General Meeting. The
        total number of all members may yet again only
        be unequal.

3.3.11 The VENTURECOMM management team may decide
        by majority vote that a certain member is weak in
        executing his/her applied skills and leadership and
        may then propose a no-confidence debate. At such
        no-confidence debates only explicit matters as con-
        cern the Organisation and its philosophy and manual
        are to be discussed or taken into consideration and
        victimisation as a result of misrepresentation or
        misunderstanding will not be permitted. Maturity has
        to be of the highest order in this instance.

3.3.12 Any disputes arising from a VENTURECOMM
        management no-confidence debate have got to be
        referred to the executive for resolution whereupon
        decisions based on the violation of Company
        philosophy and manual procedures only shall be con-
        sidered and the necessary action for a reprimand
        taken. For fair arbitration a minimum of two members
        of the executive must be present at a hearing.

3.3.13 Should a VENTURECOMM member go on leave or be absent for a few meetings, the same co-opting route as in 3.3.10 shall apply, save for the fact that the member thus co-opted only serves for the period during which the VENTURECOMM member is on leave or absent.

4.   PROCEEDINGS OF MEETINGS

4.1   A) Normal meetings

4.1.1   The Chairman of VENTURECOMM, or failing him the Vice-chairman, shall act as Chairman at every meeting. If neither the Chairman or Vice-chairman is available, VENTURECOMM members can elect a member to stand in as Chairman for that particular meeting.

4.1.2   VENTURECOMM may meet together for the despatch of business, adjourn and otherwise regulate its meetings as it thinks fit, provided it shall meet not less than twice a month.

4.1.3   With preference, a weekly meeting should be held to prioritise tasks and devise forward action plans for a week in advance and then follow up those plans at the next meeting.

4.1.4   No business shall be transacted at any meeting of VENTURECOMM unless a minimum of three members are present at such meetings.

4.1.5   General questions arising at any meeting of VENTURECOMM shall be decided by a majority of votes, each member having one vote save that in the event of an equality of votes the Chairman shall have a casting in addition to his deliberative vote. Specific Port-folio questions must be addressed as further described under item 5 (Powers).

4.1.6   Meetings need not have an Agenda but Minutes need to be placed on record in the VENTURECOMM Minutes Book for follow-up. Save for VEN-TURECOMM Meetings, VENTURECOMM itself will hold a once-a-month meeting with all staff to give feedback. At these meetings the required Agenda must be drawn up and copies of Minutes sent to Head Office as per the usual CARE Group procedures.

4.1   B) Annual General Meetings

4.1.7   Annual General Meetings shall be held at each branch between the months of August and October of any given year but will in any event, not be later than 31 October of each year.

4.1.8   Early notice is to be given to the executive of the date of such a meeting, as well as to CARE Groups themselves.

4.1.9   At these Annual General Meetings all matters pertain-ing to the running of a branch and all operational aspects will be dealt with and the staff informed as to the year's progress.

4.1.10   At the Annual General Meetings, VENTURECOMM members will put themselves up for re-election for the ensuing year and elections will be held as under the heading Elections 3.3. To broaden the knowledge of existing Portfolio holders, it would be advisable to swop Portfolios at this time.

5.   POWERS AND AUTHORITY

5.1   Introduction

Due respect has to be given to the fact that each and every person does not have the same insight, experience, vision, knowledge and skills as far as certain aspects of the business are concerned. Certain proposed operational aspects can therefore, initially, only rest with the manager for decision-making provided the faith and trust are there that it would be executed in a <u>participative manner</u> by VENTURECOMM. It is the participative nature of VENTURECOMM which will enhance the understanding of how business functions and enhance the knowledge and skills of VENTURECOMM members enabling them to climb towards management levels.

5.2   A) Employing staff and dismissals

5.2.1   VENTURECOMM, upon agreeing by vote that a vacancy exists for a particular job and suitable applicants are there to fill the vacancy, can:

5.2.1.1 <u>Physically interview, assess and employ by vote, any person up to, but not including administrative levels (i.e. Chief Cashier, Stock Control Clerks, Goods Receiving Manager, Sales Co-ordinator, Receptionist and End Controller).</u>

<u>The Manager however retains the right initially to interview all administrative staff but will extend to VENTURECOMM members the courtesy of joining in the interview as an exercise in learning.</u>

5.2.2 VENTURECOMM can, upon recognising <u>any</u> anti-company behaviour or anti-company loyalty by any staff member, including administrative staff, put forward a proposal to reprimand any staff member at the branch within the context of Organisation Philosophy and manual. A majority vote as to the decisions taken will be binding. This does <u>not</u> apply to VENTURECOMM members themselves where the matter should be treated as in 3.3.11 and 3.3.12.

5.2.3 In the event of an actual skills deficiency on the part of administrative staff, the manager must put forward his/her proposal to VENTURECOMM for decision-making in as far as a dismissal is concerned. VENTURECOMM's majority vote will be binding after considering all the facts.

5.2.4 All dismissals must be viewed in the context of laid down Organisational Philosophy and manual and not based on cultural, sexual, religious or other misinterpretable issues. If any staff member feels that he has been unjustly dismissed by VENTURECOMM, he can appeal to the executive for arbitration. (See CARE violation and Fair Trial — Quality of Worklife Portfolio).

5.2.4.1 Arbitration can only justly and fairly be executed with a minimum of two executive members doing the arbitration.

5.2 B) Working conditions, safety, etc.

5.2.5 Any change for the enhancement of working conditions must be decided upon by majority vote of VENTURECOMM.

5.2.6 Any proposed changes, should they involve capital expenditure, must be considered and discussed within the total context of the financial affairs of the branch. At all times must wisdom prevail to consider the greater good of the greater whole, i.e. staff welfare versus branch budget performance.

5.2 C) Organisational and labour matters

5.2.7 VENTURECOMM can determine the branch's destiny by vote as to organisational and labour matters.

5.2.8 Wisdom must be applied to VENTURECOMM in as far as workload spread is concerned and due consideration must at all times be given to:

* Interpersonal relationships of various staff members.
* Productivity versus sales and performance.
* Complexity of the job at hand and skills displayed by the staff member involved.
* Days off and other work disruptions.

5.2 D) Quality of worklife, sales and merchandising, etc.

5.2.9 VENTURECOMM has the power to vote for improved quality of worklife with due consideration again being given to all possible financial expenditure that needs to be incurred.

5.2.10 Any decision that needs to be made has to be carefully weighed in its importance viz. the greater good of the greater whole.

5.3 Participative management

5.3.1 Participative management is VENTURECOMM's avenue for the lifting of levels of aspirations and for the eventual enhancement of its members' skills to run a branch effectively. We know this will be a slow process at first and the spirit of maturity with which this participative management is executed will determine our effectiveness as professional people.

5.3.2 No figures, results, reports or any other operational company information is to be held back from VENTURECOMM members. All aspects of the business, such as margins, sales, stockholding, etc. must be raised for discussion at VENTURECOMM meetings and digested.

5.3.3 Active decision-making on these matters might elude VENTURECOMM at first because of a lack of experience, but as the years go by and effective training is given, VENTURECOMM could be very involved in the day-to-day running of the operational matters of a branch.

5.4 Organisational management

5.4.1 The manager, being the most skilled at this stage with organisational matters can, without putting to vote, make an important decision on behalf of the company in as far as operational matters and philosophy are concerned.

5.4.2 Although the manager has this "exclusive" domain, he must still inform VENTURECOMM as to why he chose a certain route, e.g. cutting price, making a mark-up, spending money on advertising, making a donation, etc. so that other members can learn his reasoning.

5.4.3   VENTURECOMM however still retains the right, that should the manager transgress any area of procedure as per the manual or as per our philosophy, to proceed with a vote of no-confidence and refer it to the executive. (See Items 3.3.11 and 3.3.12.)

5.4.4   As a summary we therefore see:

5.4.4.1 Operational and organisational matters as being discussed participatively.

5.4.4.2 People and staff matters as being resolved by joint decision-making.

6.   REPRESENTATION

The individual's right of fair trial as per the Quality of Worklife Portfolio (annexed hereto) is further enhanced by the fact that:

6.1   Should a staff member be a member of a recognised union, that staff member is free to choose the elected shop stewards or any other union member as his/her legal representative.

6.2   In the event of a non-union member, such staff member may elect any VENTURECOMM member or any other staff member as being his/her legal representative.

7.   REIMBURSEMENT

7.1   VENTURECOMM members hold their offices in good faith toward more effective communication and better management.

7.2 Due to the VENTURECOMM members now having some management responsibilities over and above their individual work duties, each office bearer, excluding the Manager, will receive R50,00 (Fifty Rand) per month ex gratia payment for these additional responsibilities.

7.3 Should a VENTURECOMM member however resign or be removed from office from VENTURECOMM, the ex gratia payment will fall away and monies owing will be paid on a pro-rata basis for the period that the member served on VENTURECOMM.

7.4 The R50,00 per month ex gratia payment is not part of salary and will not form part of consideration for any other company benefits such as pension, medical aid, increases, etc.

8. VENTURECOMM TRUST

8.1 Recognition of interdependence

8.1.1 We are all part of the same organisation and work towards its benefit and our benefit, mutually.

8.1.2 In a branch we are all dependent on each other to make a success of our branch — as people we need to share the load and knowledge.

8.1.3 Our common goals within the confines of organisational philosophy can only be achieved through team effort and effective understanding of our shared values.

8.2 Developing skills

8.2.1 Distrust grows out of a feeling that the employee is not capable of doing a particular job — help him to gain the necessary skills.

8.2.2 Joint decision-making and participative management will help build the skills necessary for the future survival of Cashbuild.

8.2.3 Feedback on performance is an on-going policy and all staff must know how they're performing — tell them.

8.3 Developing empathy

8.3.1 VENTURECOMM understands that if people show personal interest in each other's lives, we can look forward to building effective trust between people, never mind perceived cultural barriers.

8.3.2 We should always try to see a situation from the other man's point of view — this is a good human relations bonding tool.

8.4 Build understanding

8.4.1 We must keep on talking and listening with the "inner" ear — work closely with peers and subordinates.

8.4.2 Talk to all staff frequently about why you think the way you do. In this manner they'll understand you and learn from your reasoning.

8.4.3 Help staff understand the business from a broader perspective and get them involved.

8.5 Reveal your motivation

194

8.5.1 If you want to ask a team member to do something good for the company — be honest. Don't try and make him think it is for his own good if it isn't.

8.5.2 All team members must know how you feel about matters — good or bad. If you don't express your feelings they can't trust how you're going to react — be open.

8.5.3 Motivate people to become interested in their own work and to develop a sense of pride in the work. In this manner they'll know that you really CARE.

8.6 Communicate effectively

8.6.1 Exercise Cashbuild's open-door policy.

8.6.2 Talk straight and reveal your intentions and don't lie to staff.

8.6.3 Widen your interest by talking to your staff often. In this manner you'll develop an appreciation for his/her cultural background and be able to judge more accurately.

I, THE VENTURECOMM MEMBER ACKNOWLEDGE AND ACCEPT THE TERMS AND CONDITIONS AS SET OUT IN THE CREED OF TRUST AND HEREBY COMMIT THE VENTURECOMM MEMBERS TO ENSURE THE EFFECTIVENESS THEREOF.

SIGNED AT: .... on .... 19.........

APPENDIX 2

CARE violation and fair trial: Disciplinary action and appeal for arbitration

CARE violation and fair trial

CARE Plan Philosophy has been given to all employees to read and it is understood that all employees will acquaint themselves with the contents thereof. Thus when considering whether an employee should be dismissed or not, the greater good of the greater whole would be deemed to have implied compliance or non-compliance to the Cashbuild Philosophy and Statement of Belief. This would be the prime consideration when dismissing an employee and likewise his defence for unfair treatment and unjust dismissal.

Issues in our Philosophy which require disciplinary action if they are violated are :

A) Any outside activity or interest which creates or might appear to others to create a conflict in interest and undivided loyalty to the Company.

Example : Revealing inside trade secrets of the Company. Competitive activities actually competing or conflicting with our business. Revealing inside information to outside competitors.

In this instance a staff member may be summarily dismissed by VENTURECOMM vote.

B) Lack of pride in the work area

Such as :

i)   Absenteeism
ii) Incapability due to ill health e.g. self-inflicted problems
iii) Unpunctuality (always late for work)
iv) Sleeping on duty (due recognition to why)
v)   Poor time-keeping: leaving work without permission and unauthorised absence from work
vi) Unsatisfactory work performance

C) Unsatisfactory work performance

* Wilful disregard for procedures and failure to exercise proper CARE and attention to the extent that tasks have to be repeated unnecessarily.
* Passing time idly or failing without reasonable cause to complete a task.
* Incompetence, after checking that competence existed before employment was given or that necessary training had been given.

After written warnings have been accepted, dismissal to be given by VENTURECOMM vote.

D) Disorderly behaviour

Management frowns upon :

* Drunkenness
* Drug taking
* Insolence toward customers and other team members

* Insubordination
* Gross negligence (uncaring attitude)
* Disrespect and refusal to carry out orders
* Threatening violence, assault, etc.

Staff members can be <u>summarily dismissed</u> by VENTURECOMM vote if any of the above misdemeanours exist.

E) Shrinkage control and dishonesty

If an employee is caught in the act of stealing, prosecute and suspend him until the case is heard or give him notice with all the full benefits. If you suspect him of theft, give notice and call in the police to prove guilt and find out the facts.

VENTURECOMM's role

VENTURECOMM as a structure, cannot vote for a dismissal or reprimand unless the employee is present throughout the hearing with his/her appointed representative. VENTURECOMM must:
* Upon reprimanding an employee listen to his side of the story without interference.
* NOT jump to conclusions.
* Make sure that all members and the offenders know exactly what has been decided and said at the hearing.
* Always be fair when judging. As we say in our philosophy: ''To judge a man against a background of ill-equipped task knowledge, is not to judge him at all.''
* Remember that the objective of a hearing is to find out whether the member is guilty of an offence or not and tempers must be controlled.
* Make sure that the staff member fully understands what he is being reprimanded for and ensure that all factors are taken into consideration like length of service and his

198

progress with the company and any apparent loyalty or significant contribution made to the company.
* Upon acquainting themselves with all the facts from all the parties, they may then vote for the necessary action to be taken.

F) Arbitration

Upon an employee being dismissed and if he feels that he was unjustly dismissed, he may appeal to the executive for arbitration.

Within three days of VENTURECOMM's decision by vote the executive has to be notified of the staff member's need for appeal whereupon two members will come to the branch and listen to both sides of the story.

In the event of a staff member still having a feeling of unfair dismissal, such staff member may appeal to the Group Personnel Manager and Group Industrial Relations Manager of Metro Cash & Carry, Head Office, for arbitration.

G) Minutes

All reprisals and/or dismissals will be executed by VOTE of VENTURECOMM and a record kept in the back of the Minutes Book. The hearing will be at an extraordinary meeting of VENTURECOMM and all members must sign the disciplinary action as well as the staff member being disciplined.

APPENDIX 3

SECTION 1 : SAFETY PORTFOLIO

Staff will be required to attend a two day course in Johannesburg (dates given) where they will be taught all aspects of Safety Matters within the Cashbuild framework.

The Safety Portfolio of the VENTURECOMM member will embrace the following fields:

i)   Understanding the Safety Act

    Safety Representatives - Designation/Function
    Prohibitions   - Wage deduction, victimisation, Offences and penalties
    Safety equipment   - Goggles, boots, gloves, etc.
    Unsafe conditions / safe conditions / merchandising

ii) Safety administration

    Reporting on general standards
    Accidents
    Reporting on incidents
    Procedures

iii) General

Business concepts - Sales
                  - Stock
                  - Gross profit
                  - Expenses
                  - Nett profit

Security - The do's and dont's of Cashbuild
           Security matters
           Shrinkage control.

SECTION 2 : MERCHANDISE AND HOUSEKEEPING PORTFOLIO

Staff will be required to attend a three day course in Johannesburg (dates given) where they will be taught all aspects of merchandising matters within the Cashbuild framework.

The Merchandising Portfolio of the VENTURECOMM member will embrace the following fields :

i)   Merchandising

Grouping of merchandise
Flow of merchandise to shelves
Neatness of packing and displaying
Yard and gondola merchandising

ii) Displays

Display of specials
Rack ends
Shopping environment

iii) Promotional aspects

Marking of merchandise - colour coding
P L U boards
Clapper boards - Special posters
Competitions - customer and internal
Special leaflets, competitions

iv) Stock availability

Out of stock monitoring
New lines request
Line trending

v) General

Business concepts - Sales
                   - Gross profit
                   - Stock
                   - Expenses
                   - Nett profit

Security   - The do's and dont's of Cashbuild
                    - Security matters
                    - Shrinkage control

SECTION 3: QUALITY OF WORK LIFE PORTFOLIO

Staff will be required to attend a four day course in Johannesburg (dates given). Three four day courses will be held over this period for our geographic areas.

During the course they will be taught all aspects of our standard of quality of work life at Cashbuild.

The Quality of Work Life Portfolio of the VENTURECOMM member will embrace the following fields :

i) Building of Trust

    The Ten Commandments of Trust
    Guidelines for developing trust
    Creating a platform for total joint decision-making
    Liaising labour problem matters with the organisation
    Ensuring solving of problems and expression of opinions

ii) Productivity

    Correct employment of labour to output
    Workload planning
    Defining areas of responsibility
    Improving customer service
    Disciplinary code

iii) Team Motivation

    The Extra Mile concept
    Merit certificate
    Notes from the CEO
    CARE books (career)
    CARE books (philosophy)
    Developing team effort
    Team news distribution and interpretation
    Bonus pay-outs
    Sales competitions, etc.

iv) Workplace CARE

    Overalls
    Lockers
    Rations

Change rooms, toilet facilities, etc
General working conditions

v) General

Business Concepts - Sales
                  - Stock
                  - Gross profit
                  - Expenses
                  - Nett profit

Security   - The do's and dont's of Cashbuild
                    Security matters
                    Shrinkage control

SECTION 4 : LABOUR PORTFOLIO

Staff will be required to attend a three day course in Johannesburg (dates given) where they will be taught all aspects of labour matters within the Cashbuild framework.

The Labour Portfolio of the VENTURECOMM member will embrace the following fields:

i) Understanding the Labour Act

Hours of work - Maximum daily and weekly, meal, tea
                 intervals, etc.
Overtime   - Rates of payments, short-time, Sundays, etc.
Annual leave   - Entitlement, pay out, period, etc.
Sick leave   - Medical aspects, period for pay, etc.
Time off   - Period and non-customer violation
Termination   - Notice period, deductions, payments
Injuries   - How to handle them

ii) Insurance policy

   Accident cover
   Pension funds
   Medical, etc.

iii) Labour administration

   Take on forms/employment
   Leave forms
   Overtime sheets
   Attendance registers
   Discharge advice
   Loan applications
   Wage levels for regions
   Job categories/rates

iv) General

   Business Concepts - Sales
                     - Stock
                     - Gross profit
                     - Expenses
                     - Nett profit

   Security   - The do's and dont's of Cashbuild
                     - Security matters
                     - Shrinkage control

APPENDIX 4

Funutional Only

Corporate culture analysis

Answer all the questions on the answer sheet. Keep in mind, all that is needed is your honest and truthful opinion. You are not being asked how you think it should be, but rather how you see it.

As I see it, our Corporate Culture is:

1. for people to feel "turned on" and enthusiastic about what they are doing;
2. for individual and organisational goals to be in harmony with one another;
3. for teamwork to be neglected;
4. for organisation policies and procedures to be helpful, well understood and up-to-date;
5. for people to communicate well with each other;
6. for people to point out errors in a way that is constructive;
7. for people to blame other people for their own mistakes;
8. for people to feel they can only succeed at the expense of others;
9. for people to start a new job without having the information they need to do it well;
10. to organise and schedule time and resources effectively;
11. to merely fit people to the job rather than fitting the job to the people;
12. for people to get whatever training is needed to help them succeed in their work;

206

13. for people to avoid making decisions and to allow problems to become chronic; 2

14. to have a clear way of measuring results; 5

15. to consistently maintain the program that is made; 5

16. for change efforts to be based on sound information; 5

17. for leaders to fail to practise what they preach; 1

18. for people to care about and strive for excellent performance; 5

19. for people to approach change efforts haphazardly without taking into account all the important factors; 3

20. for people to be involved in setting their own work objectives and work methods; 4

21. for people not to have any way of measuring how well they are doing; 1

22. for people to try to work together effectively; 3

23. for organisational policies and procedures to get in the way of what people are trying to accomplish; 3

24. for people to actively seek out the ideas and opinions of others; 4

25. for people to be recognised and rewarded for excellent performance; 5

26. for people to feel responsible for doing their own jobs right so that the whole team succeeds; 4

27. for people to help each other when they are having difficulty; 4

28. for people to be clear on what they are trying to accomplish; 4

29. for needless duplication of effort to occur; 2

30. for selection and promotion practices to be fair and equitable; 5

31. to have a lot of training sessions which do not really help on the job; 5

32. to look for solutions to problems from which all people will benefit rather than solutions from which some win and some lose; 5

33. to focus on effort or talk rather than results; 2

77

5   34. for leaders to be too busy to follow up jobs they have assigned to people;

4   35. for people to avoid blame placing, and instead, to look for constructive approaches to change;

5   36. for leaders to be concerned equally about people and performance issues;

4   37. for people to care about doing their best;

3   38. for people to approach change by dealing with real causes of problems and not just symptoms;

2   39. for people to feel "turned off" by their work in the organisation;

5   40. for people to be getting feedback on how they are doing so they can develop as individuals in a planned way;

4   41. for each person to have an opportunity to be a member of a functioning effective team;

5   42. to regularly review organisational policies and procedures and make changes when they are necessary;

4   43. for people to practise effective two-way communication;

3   44. for each person to assume responsibility for improving his/her performance;

5   45. for people to treat each other as people and not just "a pair of hands";

4   46. for people to define goals clearly;

3   47. for some people to be overworked while others have nothing to do;

5   48. for new people to be properly orientated to the job;

2   49. for decisions to be made in a haphazard way;

4   50. for leaders to help their work team members succeed;

2   51. for improvements to be only temporary;

1   52. for people involved in change efforts to focus on promises rather than results;

5   53. for leaders to be continually trying to improve their leadership skills;

3   54. for people to take pride in their own work and the work of their organisation;

5   55. for people to follow through programs that they began;

83

56. for people to feel really involved in the work of the organisation; 5

57. for people to regularly plan their work goals and review progress towards their accomplishment; 5

58. for people who work together to meet regularly to deal with important issues and to focus on ways of improving performance; 4

59. for people to view policies and procedures as things to be "worked around" or avoided; 2

60. for leaders not to notice what people do unless they do it wrong; 1

61. for people to assume responsibility for what happens in the organisation; 3

62. for people to give and receive feedback in helpful ways; 5

63. for people to know exactly what their job requires; 4

64. for a leader to make the best use of the work time available in his/her work group; 4

65. for new people to have to "sink or swin" in order to learn their jobs; 1

66. when something goes wrong to blame someone else rather than do something about it; 4

67. for leaders to demonstrate their own commitment to what the organisation is trying to accomplish; 4

68. for leaders to "dilly-dally" on decisions to be made resulting in slow decision-making; 4

69. for a spirit of teamwork to be felt throughout the organisation; 4

70. for people to focus on problems rather than on results to be achieved: 2

71. for rivalry to exist in the group which gets in the way of achieving results; 2

72. for people to emphasise the negative rather than the positive in assessing performance; 3

73. for people to meet together only when they have gripes to share; 4

74. for the leaders to be unapproachable; 2

63

75. for the people to be slack in the follow up of given tasks;
76. for the people to think that there is no scope for advancement within the organisation;
77. for a negative approach to exist amongst peers that being a cash and carry builders' merchant hampers personal career growth;
78. for the organisation to be a dynamic body;
79. for people to know exactly where they stand in as far as their growth is concerned;
80. for people to have a sense of belonging according to the organisational goals of the company.

$100 \frac{9}{6}$ $-re$ $100 +ve$

400 80

270

$= 60 \frac{9}{6} -re.$

CORPORATE CULTURE ANALYSIS ANSWER SHEET

	Strongly Agree	Agree	Undecided	Disagree	Strongly Disagree		Strongly Agree	Agree	Undecided	Disagree	Strongly Disagree
1						21					
2						22					
3						23					
4						24					
5						25					
6						26					
7						27					
8						28					
9						29					
10						30					
11						31					
12						32					
13						33					
14						34					
15						35					
16						36					
17						37					
18						38					
19						39					
20						40					

CORPORATE CULTURE ANALYSIS ANSWER SHEET

	Strongly Agree	Agree	Undecided	Disagree	Strongly Disagree		Strongly Agree	Agree	Undecided	Disagree	Strongly Disagree
41						61					
42						62					
43						63					
44						64					
45						65					
46						66					
47						67					
48						68					
49						69					
50						70					
51						71					
52						72					
53						73					
54						74					
55						75					
56						76					
57						77					
58						78					
59						79					
60						80					

APPENDIX 5
Examples of awards, memo's and publications

THE Cashbuild ORGANIZATION

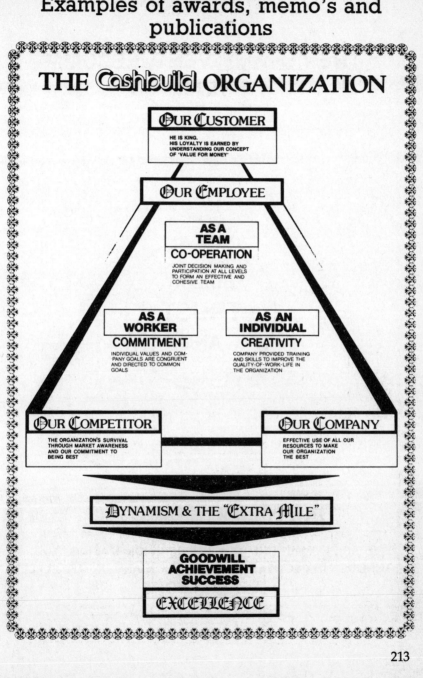

OUR CUSTOMER
HE IS KING.
HIS LOYALTY IS EARNED BY
UNDERSTANDING OUR CONCEPT
OF 'VALUE FOR MONEY'

OUR EMPLOYEE

AS A TEAM
CO-OPERATION
JOINT DECISION MAKING AND
PARTICIPATION AT ALL LEVELS
TO FORM AN EFFECTIVE AND
COHESIVE TEAM

AS A WORKER
COMMITMENT
INDIVIDUAL VALUES AND COM-
PANY GOALS ARE CONGRUENT
AND DIRECTED TO COMMON
GOALS

AS AN INDIVIDUAL
CREATIVITY
COMPANY PROVIDED TRAINING
AND SKILLS TO IMPROVE THE
QUALITY-OF-WORK-LIFE IN
THE ORGANIZATION

OUR COMPETITOR
THE ORGANIZATION'S SURVIVAL
THROUGH MARKET AWARENESS
AND OUR COMMITMENT TO
BEING BEST

OUR COMPANY
EFFECTIVE USE OF ALL OUR
RESOURCES TO MAKE
OUR ORGANIZATION
THE BEST

DYNAMISM & THE "EXTRA MILE"

GOODWILL ACHIEVEMENT SUCCESS

EXCELLENCE

THE Cashbuild VENTURECOMM TEAM

OPERATIONS

MERCHANDISING

QUALITY OF WORK LIFE

EFFECTIVE TWO-WAY COMMUNICATION

BUILDS
TRUST
AND

THE UNDERSTANDING OF INTER-DEPENDENCE

SAFETY

LABOUR

Your Growth is our Concern

CREATIVITY COMMITMENT CO-OPERATION

WE ARE COMMITTED TO JOINT DECISION MAKING
THROUGH EFFECTIVE COMMUNICATION AND UNPARALLELED
TEAM EFFORT

214

The Cashbuild Customer Creed

Statement of Belief:

We offer VALUE FOR MONEY

Quality merchandise as needed by the customer when he requires it at a realistic price backed up by impeccable service in a pleasant shopping environment with sufficient displayed information to help with his purchasing decision

Statement of Action:

Our CUSTOMER IS KING

- OUR CUSTOMER ... is the most important person in our business
- OUR CUSTOMER ... is part of our organisation — not an outsider
- OUR CUSTOMER ... is the life blood of our business
- OUR CUSTOMER ... is not dependent on us — we are dependent on him
- OUR CUSTOMER ... is not an interruption of our work — he is the purpose of it
- OUR CUSTOMER ... deserves the most courteous and attentive treatment we can give him
- OUR CUSTOMER ... is not someone with whom to argue or match wits
- OUR CUSTOMER ... is not a cold statistic — he is a flesh and blood human being with feelings and emotions like our own
- OUR CUSTOMER ... does us a favour when he calls — we are not doing him a favour by serving him
- OUR CUSTOMER ... is a person who brings us his wants and needs — it is our job to fill those wants and needs.

TRUST US FOR YOUR PROFIT

215

𝕴 am a
Cashbuilder because

* **Cashbuild** is the best Company to work for.

* **Cashbuild** C●A●R●Es about ME.

* **Cashbuild** recognises my abilities and doesn't just pay lip service to them.

* **Cashbuild** is committed to my career, well-being and growth.

* **Cashbuild** exercises a policy of joint decision making - I really can participate in the affairs of the Company.

* **Cashbuild's** management team has an Open Door Policy - they make me feel fulfilled because they really listen to me.

* **Cashbuild** is an action Company. It solves problems now.

* **Cashbuild** has direction. It knows where it is going, so therefore, I know where I'm going.

* **Cashbuild** has a secure future for me. My own abilities, and not Cashbuild's policies, will dictate my failure and success.

* **Cashbuild** is dynamic, it is my sort of Company.

Your Growth is our Concern

18/10/94

DATE   MANAGING DIRECTOR

Cashbuild
A People Company

Cashbuild

N° 0045

Certificate of merit..

This certificate is issued to _____

in respect of _____

_____

at our branch in _____

This is in pursuance of our people development policy of recognizing exceptional performance of a staff member's ability, whilst achieving the common goals of the company.

Thus done and signed at_____ on_____ 198

_____ _____
On behalf of the Company *Executive Officer*

CASHBUILD PIONEER

This serves to confirm that

*has loyally served
the Goals of the Company*
from   *to*
*and helped to build our Organization
into the Dynamic Organization it is today
and with continued diligence
will build for tomorrow*

YOU HAVE EARNED OUR TRUST
AND WE KNOW YOU CARE

———————————————
MANAGING DIRECTOR

A general memo pertaining to policy changes, views of the company, or changes in philosophy.

Whenever the C.E.O. goes on his rounds and sees anything contrary to offering value for money according to the philosophy, the incumbent is written this memo explaining the reason.
Albert the Lion is indeed unhappy.

OUR CUSTOMER IS KING! WE EARN HIS LOYALTY THROUGH OUR CONCEPT OF OFFERING **VALUE FOR MONEY** —SO...

WELL DONE!

After a Customer Focus evening or where the boss has heard of exceptional customer service in a branch, this congratulatory note is sent with an "Extra Mile" cheque.
Albert the Lion is pleased.

WE ARE COMMITTED TO TEAM EFFORT AND A POLICY OF JOINT DECISION MAKING AND PARTICIPATION AT ALL LEVELS IN ORDER TO FIND **TEAM GENERATED** SOLUTIONS TO PROBLEMS!

CONGRATULATIONS, WE'VE SEEN...

MORALE AT ITS BEST

Whenever Venturecomm is seen to be working 100% and the benefits are distinctly felt, this note is sent to the incumbents with an "Extra Mile" cheque.
Albert the Lion is pleased.

WE UNDERSTAND THAT THE MANAGEMENT OF OUR TEAM IS THAT **UNSEEN FORCE** IN TEAM SPIRIT WHICH DRIVES ALL THAT IS PHYSICAL IN THE PROCESS OF ACHIEVING **RESULTS.**

YOU'RE TURNING A DEAF EAR

It's easy for the C.E.O. to pick up the fact that there is no team spirit in a branch. The fact is that he must notice it and send out the necessary reprimand.
Albert the Lion is unhappy.

WE UNDERSTAND THAT NON-ADHERENCE TO OUR SYSTEMS IS VIEWED IN A VERY **SERIOUS LIGHT** AND IS AN INSULT TO THE ORGANIZATION – WHEN IN DOUBT AS TO HOW TO DO IT, **ASK!**

PICK UP THE PIECES AND FIX!

When Bookkeeping Department informs us of a lot of irregularities, this note is sent out to the branch.

OUR ADMIN SYSTEM AT CASHBUILD WAS DESIGNED IN ORDER TO AID US IN ASSESSING THE PERFORMANCE OF OUR ORGANIZATION AND HELPS US IN RUNNING OUR BUSINESS EFFECTIVELY WELL DONE YOU'RE A...

CASHBUILDER WHO C•A•R•E•S

No shrinkages, no system problems and good audit reports deserve this note with an "Extra Mile" cheque.
Albert the Lion is pleased.

AS PROFIT IS OUR MOTIVE, SO WE UNDERSTAND THAT CASH IS OUR LIFE BLOOD. PROFIT CONSCIOUSNESS AND GOOD STOCK MANAGEMENT SEPARATED THE **MEN FROM THE BOYS.** OUR PRIME MOTIVATOR IS TO MAKE PROFIT AND OUR LEADING MEN PUT...

MONEY IN THE BANK!

Good results, good returns on investments and good stock management are rewarded by this note and an "Extra Mile" cheque.
Albert the Lion is pleased.

Slipping on returns is reprimanded by
this note giving the reasons.
Albert the Lion is displeased.

This note is issued, listing the contravention
of the philosophy overall.

K A KIRSH GROUP COMPANY

Cashbuilder

COMMUNICATING WITH OUR CUSTOMERS

OCTOBER 1983

NUMBER 2

STATE COMES TO THE RESCUE

Cashbuild's Hall of Fame

AT Head Office in Johannesburg we have a board hanging in our entrance foyer displaying, in gold letters, the names of our exceptional people.

We are rather proud of this board, that is why it hangs in our entrance foyer — for all the world to see. We don't pay lip service to the fact that we are people orientated — we do something about it.

We really C*A*R*E for and recognition of our loyal and hard working employees.

All the company has benefitted from the recognition which they have through dedication.

Their loyalty recognition is highlighted on the attribution

6/1984

PROFIT POST

Reception

TOP REGIONAL MANAGER	
1981	G. Haumant
	G. Haumant
1982	M. Marx
	M. Marx
	M. Marx
	M. Marx
1983	K. Swan
	G. Haumant
	K. Swan
	G. Haumant
1984	K. McNulty

...made an impact on the company and they will always be honoured by the Company.

The list below displays, in category form, the names of our winning teams appearing on the Cashbuild Hall of Fame.

TOP BRANCH MANAGER	
1981	W. Wessels
	K. McNulty
1982	A. Wessels
	A. Wessels
	D. de Beer
	D. de Beer
1983	P. Olivier
	J. Marchesi
	R. Joubert
	R. Taylor
1984	I. Barton

MERITS	
1984	
P. Mthethwa	Vryheid
R. Pillay	Head Office
D. Boshoff	Maputsoe
A. Labusa	Maputsoe
C. Kheoane	Maputsoe
E. Adams	King Williams' Town
L. Maguga	Louis Trichardt
S. Masela	Louis Trichardt
G. Maswanganyi	Louis Trichardt
M. Lockie	Vryburg
D. Ramuru	Sibasa

INNOVATORS	
1984	
G. Haumant	
G. Manders	
K. McNulty	

Government projec ease ou job cris

BY PAT O'LEARY

" were not for Government projects, providing employment for workers in the construction industry, this sector of commerce would be in a horrific state with unemployment reaching astrono mical levels.

This is the opinion of Mr Ian okin, manager of PE Consulting p's Remuneration Division, aid in an interview with er that in line with other reacting to the econo on, large scale re taken place in the b had to a sy but that try to the position

n and has nt S projects said. "In tly employ 150 000 con n building new te development act

ivity has been advan the unemployed in According to Mr Hi construction compa ing areas don't norm peaks and valley counterparts in cit ket there was fa terms of demand mic depression ha ed in terms of economic depres decreased deman

While it ers to flock to of decreased d feels they wo appointed thi struction indu in a worse po else.

"T that were they would absolut se sa gene lay the tre th se h

Cashbuild TEAM NEWS

7. How has improved th medium of Vent

Cashbuild TEAM NEWS

PROFIT POST

The Great Indaba

A ten~point security plan for shopkeepers

THEY came from Francistown, Bushbuckridge, Vryheid and Kingwilliams Town. Some travelled 900 km and others only 30km. Some were weary and others again refreshed.

These were the 150-odd Cashbuilders who descended upon Johannesburg giving up their precious ___ ate time to participate i ___ ___ ___ ng the destiny of ach ___ ___ The true ach ___

The inde ___ lar ___

1. ALWAYS KEEP MONEY IN A SAFE PLACE. Even if it is only the petty cash, it must be hidden from customers and other staff members.

2. ALWAYS UNLOCK AND LOCK YOUR PREMISES YOURSELF. So often it has happened that an owner of a business has locked an employee inside knowingly or unknowingly and disaster has followed.

3. FASTEN ALL WIN-

DOWS AND ENTRANCE AND EXIT POINTS SECURELY. It easy to forget particularly in summer to close your windows and a thief can easily come and go in a few minutes.

4. DON'T ALWAYS ASSUME THAT ALL STAFF ARE AS HONEST AS YOU ARE. Take care of your property and assets or those belonging to your employer.

5. DETER PEOPLE WITH LARGE HANDBAGS

AND PARCELS. So often it has been to the detriment of the shopkeeper to allow a customer with a large handbag into his shop.

6. WATCH OUT FOR BROWSING EYES. People that loiter are normally up to no good and they are loitering and browsing in the shop to "case the joint".

7. DON'T LEAVE CONFIDENTIAL DOCUMENTATION LYING

TURN TO PAGE 2

Inside

"Most folks are about as happy as they make up their minds to be" — **Abraham Lincoln**

FEEDBACK from Venturecomm members has reflected a great variety of different opinions, suggestions and ideas. However, one thing is for sure – no branch has had an easy ride and there has been no gain with no pain.

All Venturecomm Portfolio holders responded to Albert Koopman's seven questions relating to Venturecomm and their feelings on a changing ___ th Africa.

__ questions asked were:

___ hat fears do you ___ s a leader within ___ comm?

___ do you perceive ___ onship between ___ /Venturecomm ___ Members?

___ ectively does ___ work in

___ we do to ___ e SA in

___ en. ___ and ___ en.

Cashbuild TEAM NEWS

Venture on — no pain, no gain!

Commenting on the general picture regarding lay offs Mr Hipkin said that the rampant wave of retrenchment that had swept the country since the second quarter of last year had reached a peak and it was unlikely that large scale retrenchments would continue to occur.

"The retrenchment programmes embarked upon by industry and commerce have generally been completed with most companies having ironed out problems by reach ___ mum staff le ___ for p ___

APPENDIX 6

Interface interpersonal and communication skills programme proposal for Cashbuild, 1985

CASHBUILD AND INTERFACE

Cashbuild has adopted a number of innovative and progressive philosophies which are aimed at:

- Genuine joint decision making and partipation at all levels
- The development of a cohesive team effort
- An open door policy
- Commitment to the development of people so that they are able to realise their full potential

However to ensure that these philosophies are translated into sound organisational practices it is important that all employees have the skills in the key underlying factor: dealing with people!

Interface is well placed to ensure that all Cashbuild employees have the necessary *practical communication skills*, so that the on-going implementation and success of the Cashbuild philosophies are achieved. Scientifically evaluated studies of Interface training programmes by independent researchers have indicated extremely positive results in various South African organisations. The application of Interface training at Cashbuild with its already existing positive climate will in all likelihood lead to very favourable results in implementing company policy and thereby enhancing productivity, and sound labour relations.

HOW INTERFACE WILL BE APPLIED AT CASHBUILD

The Interface training programme will be designed to meet the specific needs of Cashbuild. From initial meetings with senior

226

management it has been agreed that the Cashbuild programme will focus on three areas:

1. Management/Supervisory
2. Employee
3. Group skills (selected modules to assist Venturecomm members to function effectively as part of the team).

1. Management/Supervisory programme objective

The objective of this management programme is to provide managers with the skills to achieve maximum results through people. Managers are given practical skills to encourage participation, joint problem solving, team work and the development of the individual.

This is very much in keeping with the Cashbuild philosophy of "raising the level of manager from that of entrepeneur to true professional manager ... working together as a team through his team".

Modules

The exact modules to be included in the Management Training Programme will be finalised once the Cashbuild training needs have been established. Possible modules include:

How to:
- welcome a new employee
- give instructions
- introduce change/overcome resistance to change
- recognise dependable performance
- encourage opinions and suggestions
- respond to a complaint
- set objectives with employees
- discuss performance standards with employees
- review performance against objectives
- encourage employees to use initiative
- resolve conflict between employees

Modules such as these will assist Cashbuild managers in performing their daily managerial responsibilities in a manner that *close-*

ly reflects company policy. In addition a number of modules in this programme can be utilized to assist Venturecomm members in the carrying out of their duties, e.g. encouraging opinions, introducing changes.

2. Employee training programme

Objective

The objective of the Employee Training Programme is to provide Cashbuild employees with the necessary skills to deal effectively with typical daily interactions with Managers, Venturecomm members and fellow workers.

Furthermore this programme is designed to promote team work in a manner that is beneficial to the individual, the group and the company. It will ensure that the Cashbuild policy of "joint decision making and participation at all levels" can be implemented effectively. The training programme will provide workers with both the skills and the confidence necessary for meaningful contributions to joint decision making. This objective will be especially beneficial to Venturecomm members.

Modules

Again the final design of the programme cannot be stated until the training needs analysis is complete. Possible modules include:

How to:

  ask for help/guidance
- clarify instructions
- ask for information/explanations
- give information
- make suggestions
- express an opinion
- clarify performance standards
- ask for feedback about work performance
- co-operate in a change situation
- raise a complaint
- respond to fair/unfair criticism

3. Group skills training programme

Objective

The objective of the Group Skills Training Programme is to supplement the Management and Employee training specifically for Venturecomm groups.

The Group Skills Training Programme will consist of specialised modules in group interactions. These are likely to include:
- group problem solving/decision making
- resolving conflict in the group situation
- leading a meeting

INTERFACE AND VENTURECOMM

All three Interface programmes will be beneficial in ensuring optimal functioning of Venturecomm groups. For example from the Management Training Programme, Venturecomm members will gain skills in encouraging worker participation, introducing changes, handling complaints, etc. From the Employee Training Programme, Venturecomm members will benefit from modules such as expressing opinions, asking for information and co-operating in a change situation.

In addition, from the Group Skills Training Programme the Venturecomm group process is expected to be enhanced further.

PROPOSED ACTION PLAN FOR INTERFACE TRAINING AT CASHBUILD

The proposed Interface training programme at Cashbuild can be divided into seven sequential stages.

1. Conducting a training needs analysis

The needs analysis is undertaken to identify the most relevant modules and course content for Cashbuild. A needs analysis format and action plan will be completed in conjunction with Cashbuild. This will comprise:

(a) existing company measure, e.g. the Cashbuild corporate climate questionnaire
(b) agreed upon existing Interface measures.

The possibility of conducting a formalised research project will be discussed and finalised.

2. Selection and briefing of the project team to be involved in the programme design and development

Our experience has shown that best results are achieved when the client company is fully involved in all aspects of the programme design, development and implementation. Consequently, a project team consisting of Cashbuild employees will be selected by Cashbuild. They will work together with Interface to ensure that the programme is completely appropriate for the Cashbuild organisation, culture and company policy.

3. Design and produce Interface training programme
From (a) identified training needs; (b) ongoing advice from the Project team (c) a pool of validated Interface training material, a training programme will be designed to meet Cashbuild's needs. This process will also involve designing company specific model films unique to the Cashbuild training programmes.

4. Training Cashbuild trainers

The effectiveness of the programme is greatly increased if competent and skilled trainers conduct the training. Thus a critical aspect of the programme is the selection and training of trainers. The training of trainers will comprise 3 x 2 day modules providing trainers with the knowledge and skill required to conduct Interface training.

5. Conducting training

Interface will monitor initial training sessions. At any stage of training Interface will be available to give assistance to Cashbuild trainers.

6. Evaluating and modifying programmes

An ongoing comprehensive evaluation of Interface training programmes will be undertaken together with the company. Any necessary adjustments to the programmes will be made accordingly.

7. Follow-up

It is our policy to maintain an ongoing relationship and involvement with client companies. As such Interface undertakes to conduct regular visits to Cashbuild to ensure the ongoing success of the programme.

APPENDIX 7

Learner controlled training

GUIDELINES TO TRAINEE

This Training Manual is made up of 13 Modules which are applicable to the Imprest Stock Control System.

Each Module deals with a separate task or area of responsibility. This Manual is comprised of 13 Modules as follows:

MODULE 1 : INTRODUCTION TO THE IMPREST STOCK CONTROL SYSTEM.
           2 : CONTENT OF BLUE (TOP 100) AND BROWN IMPREST BOOKS.
           3 : SALES.
           4 : AVERAGE CYCLE SALES.
           5 : MODEL STOCK.
           6 : ORDER QUANTITY.
           7 : LEAD TIME.
           8 : TRANSFERRING ORDERS FROM IMPREST BOOK ONTO PURCHASE ORDER.
           9 : IMPRESTING OF GOODS.
        10 : HIGHLIGHTING OF PROMOTION PERIODS.
        11 : % IN STOCK ON TOP 100 LINES.
        12 : PLACING ORDERS WITH SUPPLIERS.
        13 : CONCLUSION/SUMMARY OF IMPREST STOCK CONTROL SYSTEM.

Each of the abovementioned Modules is designed according to three important learning principles. These principles ensure that learning is made easy for you. This is a Learner Controlled Training (L.C.T.) Programme which means that you control your own learning and work at your own pace. The learning principles and L.C.T. concept are explained in the pages that follow.

LEARNING PRINCIPLES

1. The objective

Each module opens with a clearly stated objective. The objective tells you what you must be able to do once you have completed the module. This means that you always have a clear picture of what is expected of you whenever you are working through any particular module of this Training Manual.

2. Details of the Module (Task) itself

The majority of each module deals with an explanation on the actual doing of the task, i.e. it explains and gives practical examples on *how to* actually perform the particular task under consideration. It also deals with aspects such as the why? (reasons for the task); where? (relevant points of reference in order to complete the task); and when? (the timing aspect of the task when this is applicable).

3. The test

At the end of each module there is a test. The tests set for each module relate directly to the objectives set and the practical examples provided

RECOMMENDED PROCEDURE FOR WORKING THROUGH THIS MANUAL

When working through this Manual you must always start at the beginning of any particular Module. In other words you must always *begin by reading the objective* and make sure that you are absolutely clear on what you will be required to do by the time that you have completed the Module. Then read through the entire Module at your *own pace*, making sure that you always understand what you are reading. You should always *ask* if you are not sure of anything.

Special attention must be given to the practical examples provided. You should work through each example slowly and thoroughly before attempting the test. Do the test once you feel confident that you have fully understood the Module covered. Remember that *the test is based on the objectives set and the practical examples provided.*

Once you have completed the test for each Module then you should give it to your Manager to mark. Your Manager has a set of model answers to all the tests. Your Manager will go over the test with you slowly and carefully so that you can learn from your mistakes if you have made any.

NB: Please remember that the purpose of the test is to help you identify the point at which you can feel sure about having mastered the necessary skill/s for any particular task.

Once you have completed a test *without error* then you can feel confident about moving on to the next Module. If you have not completed a test 100% correctly then you must redo the test (or parts of the test) until you are absolutely certain that you understand where and why you have made your mistakes. *Bear in mind that you learn through recognising and correcting your own mistakes.*

It is highly advisable to work with real examples, over and above the one provided in the manual. It is this extra little effort on your part which is going to make all the difference to your own learning and real understanding of the tasks at hand.

IT IS ESSENTIAL:

That you apply the tasks (skills) learnt to the practical on-the-job situation. Tests are not everything. The real proof of what you have learnt lies in actually being able to do the task in the real job situation. The only way to guarantee success on the job is through repeated practice. It is only practice that makes perfect. Also don't forget that *"what you do not use, you lose".*

Learner Controlled Training (L.C.T.)

This manual is a Learner Controlled Training Manual. This means that the programme has been written in such a way that *you are master or controller over your own learning.* In other words you can rely on yourself to learn the Imprest Stock Control System, by

234

taking it step by step and *at your own learning pace*. If you do encounter any problems when working through the manual, then do not hesitate to ask your Manager or even to contact Head Office if necessary. The important point is to make sure that you always get an answer to your questions.

An L.C.T. programme makes you in charge of your own learning. You are your own teacher and as such you can take full responsibility for your progress. It is your own interest and motivation that will determine your success.

Good Luck!

13/2

BIBLIOGRAPHY

Argyris, C. 1970. *Intervention theory and method*. Mass.: Addison Wesley.

Baron, R.A. 1983 *Behaviour in organizations*. Newton: Allyn & Bacon.

Bennis, W.G. 1983. *Four traits of leadership*.

Crosby, P.B. 1979 *Quality is free*. New York: McGraw-Hill.

Drucker, P.F. 1980. *Managing in turbulent times*. London: Pan Books.

Drucker, P.F. 1985. *Innovation and entrepreneurship*. London: Heinemann Ltd.

Frankl, V.E. 1959. *Man's search for meaning*. Boston: Beacon Press.

Harvard Business Review. 1978. Everyone who makes it has a mentor. (Interviews with F.J. Lunding, G.L. Clements and D.S. Perkins of the Jewel Corporation.) July-August.

Kanter, R.M. 1983. *The change masters*. Simon & Schuster.

Mintzberg, H. 1979. *The structuring of organizations*. New York: Prentice Hall.

Nasser, M.E. 1984. *Project Free Enterprise report*. Pretoria: Unisa School of Business Leadership.

Nasser, M.E., & Nel, C. 1986. Economic participation in South Africa. In *Project Free Enterprise report*. Pretoria: Unisa School of Business Leadership.

Naisbitt, J. 1985. *Reinventing the corporation*. London: MacDonald & Son.

Newman, W.M., Warren, E.K., & Schnee, J.E., 1982. *The process of management*. New York: Prentice Hall.

Peters, T.J., & Austin, N. 1985. *A passion for excellence*. London: Collins.

Peters, T.J., & Waterman, R.H. 1982. *In search of excellence*. New York: Warner Books.

Porter, L.W., Lawler, E.E., & Hackman, J.R. 1975. *Behavior in organizations*. New York: McGraw-Hill.

Ross, J.E., & Ross, W.C. 1982. *Japanese quality circles and productivity*. Virginia: Reston Publishing Co.

Schein, E.H. 1970 *Organizational psychology*. New York: Prentice Hall.

Schein, E.H., & Bennis, W.G. 1965. *Personal and organizational change through group methods*. New York: John Wiley & Sons.

Toffler, A. 1980. *Beyond the break-up of industrial society: political and economic strategies in the context of upheaval*. Williamson, J.N. pp. 9-28. Wilson Learning Corporation.

Zaleznik, A. 1977. Managers and leaders: are they different? *Harvard Business Review*. 123-139. New York: John Wiley & Sons.